Changing States

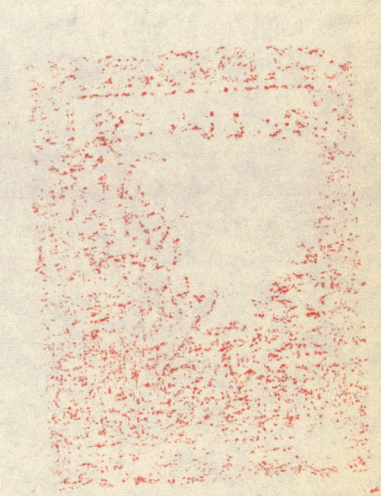

Changing States

A Labour Agenda for Europe

Glyn Ford MEP
Glenys Kinnock MEP
Arlene McCarthy MEP

Mandarin

All authors' profits from the sale of this book
will be donated to One World Action, the
overseas agency working for justice with
partners in Africa, Asia and Latin America.

A Mandarin Paperback
CHANGING STATES

First published in Great Britain 1996
by Mandarin Paperbacks
an imprint of Reed International Books Ltd
Michelin House, 81 Fulham Road, London SW3 6RB
and Auckland, Melbourne, Singapore and Toronto

Reprinted 1996

Copyright © Glyn Ford, Glenys Kinnock and
Arlene McCarthy 1996
The authors have asserted their moral rights

A CIP catalogue record for this title
is available from the British Library
ISBN 0 7493 2259 4

Typeset in 11 on 13 point Sabon
by Avon Dataset Ltd, Bidford on Avon, Warks
Printed and bound in Great Britain
by Cox & Wyman Ltd, Reading, Berkshire

This book is sold subject to the condition
that it shall not, by way of trade or otherwise,
be lent, resold, hired out, or otherwise circulated
without the publisher's prior consent in any form
of binding or cover other than that in which
it is published and without a similar condition
including this condition being imposed
on the subsequent purchaser.

Contents

Notes on contributors — vii
Acknowledgements — xiii
Authors' note — xiv
List of abbreviations — xv
Introduction: The European Paradigm *Glyn Ford* — xvii

1. Economic and Monetary Union *Alan Donnelly* — 1
2. Employment and Prosperity *Mark Hendrick* — 17
3. European Union Research and Development *Eryl McNally* — 43
4. A Europe of the Regions: Building Economic and Social Cohesion in Britain and Europe *Arlene McCarthy* — 57
5. Women in Europe *Christine Crawley* — 89
6. Racism, Residents and Refugees *Glyn Ford* — 102
7. Development Perspectives and the EU: Combating Poverty in the Global Village *Glenys Kinnock* — 126
8. European Media and Cultural Policy *Carole Tongue* — 145
9. Going Places: A European Transport Vision *Mark F. Watts* — 160
10. From Common Agricultural Policy to Rural Development Policy *David Thomas* — 173
11. Europe and the Environment *Anita Pollack* — 190
12. Protecting the Citizen as Consumer *Phillip Whitehead* — 205
13. Power to the People *David Martin* — 229
14. Developing the Brussels-Westminster Axis *Gary Titley* — 243

Further reading — 252

Notes on contributors

Glyn Ford MEP (Greater Manchester East, 1984)

Glyn Ford was originally a geologist and oceanographer. While at Manchester University's Department of Science and Technology Policy he spent a period as a visiting Professor at the University of Tokyo.

From 1989 to 1993 he was the leader of the EPLP, a member of Labour's NEC and Deputy Leader of PES.

From 1984–1986 he was the Chair of the Parliament's Committee of Inquiry into the Rise of Racism and Fascism and from 1989–90 he was the *rapporteur* for the second Committee of Inquiry. He is the European Parliament's representative on the Council of Ministers' Consultative Commission on Racism and Xenophobia, set up by François Mitterrand and Helmut Kohl in July 1994. He is the president of the European Parliament's branch of the Inter-Parliamentary Council Against Anti-Semitism and treasurer of the Anti-Nazi League.

He is a member of the editorial board of *Tribune* and Vice-President of the Labour Movement in Europe. He is a columnist for *Tribune*, *Research Fortnightly* and *Searchlight*, and the author of three earlier books: *The Future of Ocean Technology* with Chris Niblett and Lindsay Walker

(Frances Pinter, 1987), *Fascist Europe* (Pluto Press, 1992) and *Evolution of a European* (Spokesman, 1993.)

Glenys Kinnock MEP (South Wales East, 1994)

Glenys Kinnock was educated at Holyhead Comprehensive School and graduated from University College, Cardiff in 1966. She has been a teacher in secondary, primary, infant and nursery schools and has specialized in reading development. She has had a lifelong involvement in the Labour Party.

She is a Member of the Development Committee and the Youth, Media, Education and Culture Committee. She is First Vice-President of the Africa Caribbean and Pacific/European Joint Assembly.

Glenys Kinnock has published *Eritrea – Images of War and Peace*, and *Namibia: Birth of a Nation*, plus a collection of interviews with British women, *By Faith and Daring*.

Born in July 1944, Glenys married Neil Kinnock in 1967 and they have two children, Stephen and Rachel.

Arlene McCarthy MEP (Peak District, 1994)

Arlene McCarthy is elected as the EPLP and Party of European Socialist's spokesperson on regional policy.

During 1996 she has led a campaign to find out why privatized utilities were given millions of pounds of European taxpayers' money in handouts, money which could have been better used in Britain's regions to reduce unemployment and create jobs.

She is a substitute member of the Economic and Monetary Affairs Committee and participates in the PES's Employment Working Group. She is the draftsperson of the

EP report on the implementation of structural funds and regional policy in the UK.

Before her election as a Euro MP she was in charge of running European programmes at Kirklees Metropolitan Borough Council attracting substantial amounts of money. She is a former guest research fellow and lecturer in European foreign and security policy at the Free University of Berlin.

Christine Crawley MEP (Birmingham East, 1984)

Christine Crawley chaired the EP's Women's Rights Committee from 1989–1994. She is currently deputy leader of the EPLP. Christine was a drama teacher and youth theatre director before being elected to the EP. She was also a local councillor from 1989–1993. Christine is married and she has three children. Her hobbies include amateur drama and attending local football matches, and she is a Fellow of the Royal Society of Arts.

Alan Donnelly MEP (Tyne & Wear, 1989)

Before being elected, Alan Donnelly's experience included a career in the GMB trade union where he served as Regional Education Officer, followed by terms as Regional and National Finance Director. He is the PES spokesman on the Committee on Economic and Monetary Affairs and Industrial Policy and sits on the Monetary Affairs subcommittee. He is also chairman of the EP Interparliamentary Delegation for Relations with the US Congress and is actively involved in promoting transatlantic industry dialogue. In October 1991 the German government awarded him with its highest civilian honour – Knight Commander of the Order of Merit – for his work as *rapporteur* on the Parliament's Special Committee on German Unification.

Mark Hendrick MEP (Lancashire Central, 1994)

Mark Hendrick is the EPLP spokesperson on Economic and Monetary Affairs. He is a member of the Economic and Monetary Subcommittee and was a member of the Temporary Committee for Employment.

David Martin MEP (Lothians, 1984)

Working with Neil Kinnock, David Martin was instrumental in helping to change Labour's negative stance on Europe. He is a long-term campaigner on the need to address the European 'democratic deficit', and has written extensively on the need for democratic institutional reform of the EU. Widely regarded as an expert on constitutional matters in Europe, he was the author of the EP's Report on Maastricht and co-author of the Parliament's position on the 1996 IGC.

Eryl McNally MEP (Bedfordshire and Milton Keynes, 1994)

Eryl McNally is the Vice-President of the EP Committee on Research, Technological Development and Energy. She is also a member of the Parliament's Scientific and Technological Options Assessment Panel (STOA).

She is a former teacher, adviser and OFSTED inspector with wide experience in local government. She specializes in renewable energy.

Anita Pollack MEP (London South East, 1989)

Anita Pollack is Australian, has a Masters degree in political sociology from London University, and worked in book publishing and politics before being elected. She is EPLP spokesperson on the Environment in the European Parliament and an unpaid member of the Board of Global Legislators OrganiBE Europe, as well as convenor of its forest working group.

David Thomas MEP (Suffolk and South West Norfolk, 1994)

Born in Cardiff, David Thomas moved to Suffolk in 1980 to study at the University of East Anglia and, as a member of Suffolk County Council, played an active role in local politics. He is a member of the Committee on Agriculture and Rural Development and a substitute member of the Foreign Affairs Committee. He is the EPLP spokesperson on Agriculture and Rural Development.

Gary Titley MEP (Greater Manchester West, 1989)

Gary Titley is a member of the Foreign Affairs and External Economic Relations committees. He is a member of the NEC of the Labour Party's Domestic and International Policy Subcommittee. He was also a member of the Party's Plant Committee on electoral reform.

Carole Tongue MEP (London East, 1984)

Carole Tongue is PES spokesperson for Media, Culture, Youth and Education policy. She specialises in industrial policy, labour relations and constitutional affairs. Her priority is legislation to strengthen the European Audio-visual Industry working with entertainment unions, producers, writers and directors. She is also a Council Member of Charter 88.

Mark Watts MEP (Kent East, 1994)

Mark Watts was born in Bermondsey in 1964 and educated at Maidstone Grammar School and the London School of Economics where he secured a Master of Science degree in economics. He was elected to the Maidstone Borough Council in 1986, where he became Labour Group Leader four years later. He worked briefly for the GLC and was employed by the Royal Borough of Kingston-upon-Thames until his election to the EP. He is a member of the EP Transport and Tourism Committee and Transport spokesperson for the EPLP.

Philip Whitehead MEP (Staffordshire East and Derby, 1994)

Philip Whitehead is Chair of the EP's Consumer Intergroup and member of the Environment, Public Health and Consumer Protection Committee. He was previously MP for Derby North. He was Chair of the Consumer's Association from 1990–94, but writes here in a personal capacity.

Acknowledgements

We would like to thank Gwilym Jones, Sarah Chilton, Katie Robbins, Kay Baxter and Nicky McCann for their patience and time in the protracted period which was required to complete the book.

Authors' note

Within nine months the Labour Party will have its last best hope of power in a generation. When Labour left office in 1979 the European Parliament was not even directly elected and the Common Market was writ small in our politics. Today it is clear that the European Union is central to our future. To try to halt the forward march of Europe is like late-eighteenth century politicians asking for a pause in the Industrial Revolution. Revisionist historians claim King Canute was merely trying to demonstrate the limits of sovereign power with his futile appeal to the tide. No one can use that defence for the Tory nationalists threatening a withdrawal from the Union.

Simultaneous with Tony Blair arriving in 10 Downing Street, Labour ministers will arrive in Brussels. The volume of work to be done is now all too clear. The BSE-inspired veto of all Council proposals saw seventy-seven Community actions vetoed across nine Council Meetings in a period of twenty-three days. At this rate it would mean that in the new government's first hundred days, Labour would have to make decisions on over 350 EU proposals shaped by a government thrown out of office by a disgruntled electorate.

Here, a group of Labour MEPs offer a political map of the European labyrinth for Labour to use both as a guide after the election and as a tool with which to handle the decision mountain.

Abbreviations

ECU	European Currency Unit
EFTA	European Free Trade Area
EPLP	European Parliamentary Labour Party
ESF	European Social Fund
EU	European Union
GDP	Gross Domestic Product
IGC	Intergovernmental Conference
MECU	ECU one million
NEC	National Executive Committee
NIESR	National Institute of Economic and Social Research
OECD	Organisation for Economic Cooperation and Development
PES	Party of European Socialists
TENs	Trans-European Networks

GLYN FORD
Introduction: The European Paradigm

The European Union is not primarily the product of politicians. The single European Market was neither invented by Jacques Delors, nor built in his image. Too many believe that this is, and was, the case. True, the European Community's original *raison d'etre* was political: to bind the economies of Europe's formerly warring nations together so tightly that another European war was inconceivable. Political will was to be the motor of economic integration. Yet after Coal, Steel and Atomic Energy Communities, the economic enterprise languished as political will ebbed.

What drove integration forward again were not political imperatives but economic ones. By the early eighties a single market was being formed sector by sector within the bounds of the European Economic Community, as thousands of businessmen and women, managers, scientists and entrepreneurs recognized that the only way to compete with Japan and the United States was through the enlargement of the home market to a truly continental scale. By design or accident, leading European companies, from ICL to BMW, from British Aerospace to ENI, Europeanized their operations. Industrial Union was built piece by piece, far removed from the traditional political processes.

It became clear that the European nation state was both too small to deal with global issues and too large to deal with local and regional problems. The future had to be European; and the European Community the forum within which this future could be developed.

The challenges, contradictions and uncertainties which we now face demand shared policies. We need to pool our resources in the interests of mutual co-operation and mutual benefit. Late capitalist industry needs the firm foundations of a large domestic market.

An Industrial Revolution

Europe's Industrial Union was a 'natural' development. It would have taken place without the Single European Act, Maastricht, the Delors programme or the Commission's 1988 White Paper. Yet on its own, this new market would have had neither safeguards nor controls.

There is a parallel between what has happened in Europe in the last few years and what happened at the time of the Industrial Revolution two centuries ago. Then, the aggregation of British industry led to a rapid transformation from regional to national level. In 1992 we moved, in another quantum leap, from national to European level. The former transformation led to massive regional misery, as poverty and deprivation followed. Economic and industrial union, as history shows, does not automatically produce a better standard of living or open up new opportunities for all its citizens.

The only way to prevent adverse consequences is to ensure that certain social and political counterweights are put in place – an absolutely crucial task for the European left. This is what is meant by the 'social dimension': it is not merely a form of damage limitation, of reducing the impact of the economic change that results from the creation of a single European market; rather, it is central to the success of the Union.

The necessary corollary to economic and industrial union is a strong regional and industrial policy. We have to ensure that the regions are supported and that our industries thrive: we simply cannot afford the cost of unemployment, poverty and the overall underperformance that will otherwise follow.

These countervailing forces are already in place within the European Community. The European Regional Development Fund (ERDF) targets the declining and peripheral areas, providing support to regions outside the 'golden triangle' of Brussels, Frankfurt and Milan for productive investment in small, medium and larger enterprises and transport infrastructure. The European Social Fund (ESF) provides resources for training and retraining the unemployed throughout the Union in order to ensure that a trained workforce is available for the emerging industries of the future. The new Objective 4 programme complements ESF funding with its 'retain and retrain' measures, giving the possibility of financial support to companies in high-skill production so that they can retrain their workforce to use the newest technologies. However, a myopic British Conservative Government refused to see the benefits of these new programmes and, in effect, opted out.

If we fail to develop policies for economic and social cohesion, the European Union will replicate all the worst aspects of industrial society: pockets of poverty and deprivation; areas of high unemployment alongside areas of near full employment; some regions in permanent decline and disintegration while, alongside them, others expand in wealth and power.

Instead, we must put measures in place which prevent 'core' areas overheating and encourage business and industry to flourish in the more peripheral regions. The Cohesion Fund is the nation-state equivalent of regional aid, designed to help the European Union's four poorest member states meet the convergence criteria for Economic and Monetary Union (EMU). It allows them to continue to pay for large-scale transport and environmental schemes with European grants of up to 80%, while reining in public deficits to meet EMU.

The European Commission's task is to steer Europe through these difficult industrial, economic and political transformations. The essential dangers are illustrated very simply in E.P. Thompson's *The Making of the English Working Class*. Two centuries ago, with the emergence of English Industrial Union, the arrival of new technologies slashed the workforce in competitive firms while placing the remaining workers under new, fiercer labour disciplines and putting the uncompetitive firms and their workers out of business. The peripheral regions lost out badly. The railways took away as much prosperity as they brought, and villages and towns lost out to the cities. People moved to the major conurbations – Manchester, Birmingham and London – in huge numbers, bringing prosperity to few and poverty to many. All this and more now threatens at a European level.

Industrial Restructuring

All sectors of industry in Europe are in the process of restructuring. An example is provided by the arms industry – which theoretically is protected from the demands of the single market, since the Treaty allows for each country's 'national security considerations' to be put first. In the past decade, however, two events have had huge repercussions for the industry, and reinforced the demands of the single market: firstly, the end of the Cold War and secondly, the Gulf War. Arms manufacturers have effectively been forced towards merger and amalgamation.

The consequence will be the loss of hundreds of thousands of jobs over the coming decade. The impact will be devastating. Nevertheless, Europe must try to keep the 'skill teams' of scientists and engineers employed in the defence sector intact so that they can provide the technological dynamic for the new industries of the future. Well-funded sectoral programmes, similar to those promoted by the Labour Party in their arms diversification proposals, will help us adapt to this post-Cold War Europe.

Almost identical considerations drive the evolution of Europe's other major industrial sectors. Millions of jobs are under threat.

Increasing Competitiveness

On the face of it, the European Union's position looks strong. Europe has the biggest markets and a large pool of scientific skills. The reality, however, is somewhat different. Industrial growth has slowed, unemployment is already approaching twenty million, and in many sectors Europe is being out-competed by the USA and Japan. A major cause of this is Europe's low level of spending on Research, Development, and Demonstration (RD&D) and general industrial investment compared with its main competitors. Follow-on research to exploit the secondary spin-off from technical innovation is weak and venture capital is short. To compound these problems, there is little real co-ordination between European states, leading to duplication and waste of resources in some areas and to gaps in others.

This is a matter of utmost concern. Europe's political regeneration will ultimately be determined by its economic performance. A competitive industry, whether manufacturing or service, needs advanced technologies. These technologies depend to a significant extent on the quality and quantity of RD&D. There is therefore a need for a larger and more coherent research programme within the European Union, linked to a Community industrial policy. The former has to move away from the Dan Dare technologies of the past, from the emphasis on nuclear fission and fusion and high energy physics, towards research that is directly relevant to the market, leading to innovation, improved competitiveness and profit. Sciences such as biotechnology and gene therapy, information technology and plate tectonics are more relevant to Europe's future than the electro-mechanical technologies of Star Wars. Europe's highly successful collaboration with Japan's Human Frontier Science Programme is more valuable than the promised global partnership from fusion research.

The European Union's research centres, such as Ispra, are paradigms of academic under-achievement and intellectual nostalgia. This must be changed: research that is not making the grade should not receive European Community subventions. Europe can no longer be the funder of the last resort; rather it should lead the pack.

Where's the Money From?

New programmes and policies require both financial resources and political will. The only major internal source of funds is the Common Agricultural Policy (CAP), which currently consumes 48% of the European Union budget and which is in urgent need of reform. Substantial and sustained reform of the CAP must be undertaken to release funds for more economically productive use. Yet European governments have so far failed to undertake radical change to agriculture expenditure: 85% of the budget is now fixed until 1999. The BSE debacle will not make the situation any easier; nor will the current revolution in biotechnology, which is bringing further increases in productivity. There will not be an opportunity to redress the imbalance by bringing agricultural spending under control and targeting it more carefully until the new millenium. It is essential that when this opportunity arrives it is fully exploited by a British Labour Government.

Further funds must be found elsewhere. There is currently little if any support in Member States for an increase in contributions to the European Union budget. Yet most want more for less. There is support, for example, for the enlargement of the European Union, but this would require an estimated 60% increase in the budget, raising Member States' contributions from 1.2% to over 2% of their total GNP. Meanwhile, measures already under consideration in the current budget, geared towards improving competitiveness and combating unemployment, would require a doubling or tripling of research funds from their current 4% of the Community budget.

Reform of the budget is essential if the challenges of enlargement and EMU are to be met and the fight against unemployment is to be effective. We must make better use of current resources and combat fraud. But these measures, on their own, will not be enough. New resources are vital to the task of tackling Europe's future challenges.

Political Will

Political will, too, is essential – yet even more difficult to secure. Many Member States, and many representatives in national parliaments, still believe the nation state to be the most desirable and practical area for action on the crucial issues. Yet, in reality, the ability of each nation state to pursue effective national policies has been severely constrained by structural changes in the international system and the globalization of economic forces and capital flows which has taken place over the last few years.

Europe is not yet properly democratic. National parliaments have failed to come to terms with the evolution of industrial society, and as a result, democratic powers that were fought for and won over the last century have been meekly surrendered at a European level. The elected European Parliament is undermined by a semi-detached, appointed Commission and a Council of Ministers which meets in secret, and which until recently has refused even to publish minutes of its proceedings.

Political will can best be guaranteed by strengthening the legitimacy of the European Union in the eyes of European citizens. If citizens and residents are not persuaded of the value of working together in Europe, then there will be little support for the European project. It is up to politicians to engage and persuade people. They have to show that Europe can be a force for social stability and job creation, for consumer and social protection, for high environmental standards, balanced development and for international solidarity, human rights and peace.

The Social Framework

Europe has to create the social framework for a high-wage, high-skill, high-technology society. We need legislation on hours of work, on the minimum wage, holidays, maternity and paternity leave. We need legislation to protect part-time and temporary workers, night workers and trans-frontier workers, women and child workers. We need stronger and better health and safety legislation for the workplace and the home. We need to ensure equal treatment for all, no matter what sex, race or nation. We need the Social Chapter, which Labour is pledged to sign.

Such a framework will not emerge by accident: it will have to be fought for by Labour and the European left. But we do have allies. In Italy, the historic victory of the left in April 1996 after half a century of waiting will provide us with a new partner. Equally, in northern Europe, the majority of parties of the centre right recognize that they cannot allow labour-intensive industry to drift to the low-wage parts of the community. These parties will travel with us for part of our political journey, even if they may want to alight before our final destination. It remains for the European left to ensure that progress is made towards the construction of a Social Europe, alongside single market legislation and EMU.

This framework must be put in place before there is any further enlargement of the European Union: deepening the Community has to be given priority over widening it. It is necessary to strengthen the Union's internal institutional procedures first: with more new member states the existing system would collapse, and the policy gains of the 1990s would be lost. We must offer a strong commitment to the countries of Central and Eastern Europe as they make the painful transition to democracy, but not at the expense of our own hard-won gains. The British Conservatives' enthusiasm for rapid enlargement is aimed at undermining the political and social aspects of the Union, in order to return to a free market: a free-for-all, with gross inequalities in living standards and employment levels.

Britain and the Single Currency

EMU and a single currency must remain firmly on the agenda. Without a single currency the single market will be strained and contorted, and capital-intensive activity within the Union will be drawn towards the low interest rate regions. Equally, in the absence of a single currency, forward purchasing becomes less a choice of choosing the best supplier and more a gamble on the direction and scale of future currency movements. Marginal price differences as an impulse for improved competitiveness are swamped by the lottery of the currency markets. Britain cannot go it alone outside a single currency.

Member states can expect to benefit from the reductions in transaction costs, the elimination of exchange rate risks and the stable interest rates which would follow EMU. Speculative gambling on the currency markets by city speculators in scenarios like Black Wednesday would be avoided. However, member states must deploy a budgetary strategy in the run-up to EMU which avoids drastic cuts in spending in poorer regions and on education, training and basic infrastructure. Employment targets are as important for cohesion as budgetary deficits and inflation.

The promised referendum on Europe will be unnecessary if the choice at the General Election is clear. However, if a referendum is decided on, it must be Labour who set the question, and not the Tories: do we go forward with the rest of Europe, or do we get left behind?

Britain's Record

Britain's relationship with Europe has been described as the politics of calculated distance. Time and again the Tories have tried to stall moves towards Economic and Monetary Union by pleading Britain's unique economic circumstances. English exceptionalism has been the guiding principle of British European policy since the war. British accession to the EEC in 1972 was less motivated by a commitment to Europe than by fear.

Since Britain failed to join the single market at the beginning, Europe's design was left to France and Germany, while Britain was relegated to the role of spectator. The last two decades of Conservative policy in Europe have been characterized by spoiling tactics to block new initiatives. The only area in which the Conservatives have wanted to speed up progress has been that of securing budgetary rebates. Now, with Tory Eurosceptics on the rampage, many believe that the Conservatives' real goal after the General Election will be an effective withdrawal from further integration. The wilder elements in the party want to go even further and re-open the political settlement of the referendum in 1975. This would be a tragedy for Britain.

The saga of Britain's role in Europe is one of squandered potential, misguided policies and mismanagement of resources. Compared with our European partners, Britain has a poor record in everything, from welfare rights to workers' rights, from environmental protection to social provision. The strains and divisions in the Conservative Party over Europe prevent a Conservative-led Government from delivering the best deal for Britain. Margaret Thatcher parted company with five Ministers over the issue of Europe and was eventually brought down by it herself. John Major's experience is too painful to retell.

As a result we are being left behind in Europe. The Thatcher/Major years have given us a twin legacy of skill shortages and declining educational standards. The abilities of the entrepreneur to give British industry a boost cannot be relied upon without the foundation of a skilled workforce. In Germany, 85% of 16–18 year olds are in some form of training. It is not surprising that the proportion of UK businesses going bust is inordinately high. What is it, then, that the Conservative Government has been seeking to maintain by limiting our involvement in Europe? What great British achievement are we afraid of losing or compromising?

Britain has failed to develop a vision of a European future for its citizens. The policy, if it can be called a policy, has consisted of a series of knee-jerk negative responses to the initiatives of other states in the Community: at best a passive 'don't know', at worst a plain 'no'. What is needed is an active 'yes'. Britain has not taken enough pains to co-operate with and engage in dialogue with its European partners. Instead Britain has stood back and criticized plans, drawn up by others, already on the table. It may not be necessary to have a grand design or utopian vision, but it is necessary to have clear objectives, and to want to influence the future development of a community of which we have been a member for two decades.

Europe's Role on the World Stage

Voices in the Conservative Party argued that European disunity over the Gulf and Bosnia and the Community's consequent failure to find a common position meant that there was now no point in attempting to establish a common Foreign and Security policy. The logical conclusion of this view is that Britain is once again free to try to consolidate its transatlantic relationship, which was temporarily restored during the Gulf War. These people are not living in the real world. The United States is increasingly looking inwards. When it does look outwards, its political and economic interests turn it across the Pacific to Japan rather than across the Atlantic to the UK or Europe. Europe has to stand on its own feet and speak with one voice or we will not be heard at all.

Once industrial and social union, economic and monetary union are established, the next phase will be to move towards a Common Foreign and Security Policy and a Security and Defence Union. This final goal is a long way off, but we should be ready to move forward. Once we have common industrial and economic interests, the Union's foreign policy interests will inevitably converge. Clearly the burden of the past will continue to have its influence over individual member states, whether it be France's historical role in Africa, Spain's in Latin America or Germany's in Central and Eastern Europe. Yet in the end, foreign policy is a derivative of economic interests. The Union can either take a lead, or allow itself to be buffeted to and fro on the world stage by the decisions of the United States and Japan.

Like it or not, we are going to see Europe without America. In the past, Britain's 'special relationship' with the United States has compromised our position in Europe. Britain's nostalgia for its status as a great power (or, at worst, the delusion that it still has this status) has been a major obstacle to a proper role within Europe. Britain has trained to be first among equals. But with the end of the Cold War, US and European economic interests have diverged sharply and will continue to do so. No amount of wishful or wistful thinking can change this.

Labour in Europe

Labour's opposition to Europe in the past stemmed from the idea that it represented merely a Common Market, and not a Community. Labour does not now harbour any illusions that Britain's future will be anything other than European. Most people are now exposed to the culture and languages of our European neighbours: more and more, our supermarkets are filled with French and German produce, our high streets with Italian design and our airwaves with Continental football. Many British graduates are beginning to look for jobs on the Continent, where they are paid more for their skills.

Attitudes in Britain are slowly changing. Although wild Euro-enthusiasm is limited, few Britons, in their heart of hearts, see any alternative to our continued membership of and full participation in the European Union. The more exchange we have with European partners, the more we are able to compare living and education standards and the more we realize that those in Britain are in decline.

The British left has in the past been guilty of both parochialism and the same English exceptionalism, and slow to recognize the political implications of global competition married to a genuine internationalism. This is no longer the case: with the socialists setting the agenda in the European Parliament, the European Parliamentary Labour

Party is working to continue to change Europe from a narrow business and financial community to a genuinely democratic, economic, social and political community. A strong commitment to Europe does not involve abandoning British culture; nor does it involve renouncing national sovereignty. There is ample room for a national dimension in the practice of subsidiarity, even if the Tories distort the meaning of the term.

A small 'National Socialist' faction persists within the Labour Party, arguing that we took a wrong turn into Europe, that if we could only go into reverse and back up, we would go merrily on our way. In one magic bound Labour would be free to pursue growth and prosperity alone. Their grasp of history has to be questioned. For the last century and a quarter, the British economy has been in slow decline. From the high point of the mid-nineteenth century, when Britain ruled the waves and wrote the rules, it has been downhill all the way. Today we are the fifth poorest country in a European Union of fifteen Member States.

Weak national or regional economies can only survive against stronger partners by accepting lower living standards, diminished rights for workers and trade unions, higher unemployment and the export of its best workers. Pooling what we have with other European countries and economies, on the other hand, will give us more power and more control over our destiny, restoring our competitiveness. Britain hasn't had sovereignty in the Eurosceptic sense of the term for at least three-quarters of a century.

Britain's options in the future depend upon our ability to adjust to the changing world economy. Small and medium-sized countries need to work together in larger regional groupings to make their joint 'national' economy viable. Britain has an even more extensive shift to make than our

European partners if it is to become a modern industrialized West European state: our capitalist revolution, being the first, never really reached completion. The main obstacle to a thorough modernization of Britain, moreover, is cultural: our society still suffers from a basic hostility towards technology and engineering (and hence innovation), and consequently from ineffective management. We have much to learn.

The market has the prime role to play in the modernization and Europeanization of Britain, but it must be guided and regulated according to our social and economic needs. Competitive forces can be channelled and directed. In Japan, the Ministry of International Trade and Industry (MITI) stimulates competition between companies and controls demand, as well as directing finance and investment. This partnership between government and industry underpins the Japanese economy. Only in Britain is it taken as axiomatic that public investment and government intervention is bad.

Regionalization is one answer to meeting the aspirations of the British people: allowing them to organize and govern their own affairs. Devolution for Scotland and Wales, and regional governments in England, would provide channels for economic regeneration which could not be countenanced by a remote and overburdened central government. It is important that local, regional and national structures all have their place within the European Union, and that decisions continue to be taken at the appropriate level.

A European future under a Labour Government offers British people a vast improvement on the quality of life of the past seventeen years. The 'freedom' of the Thatcher and Major years was the freedom for business to make money at the taxpayers' expense. Quality of life cannot be measured simply in material goods: our freedom has to include a freedom from racial and sexual discrimination and from environmental pollution; a freedom to enjoy good health and the right to education and training.

Labour must seize the agenda, not only in Britain, but also in Europe. It will be up to a Labour Government to harness Europe's dynamism to help Britain achieve its future industrial, economic, social, political and security goals. Britain under Conservative rule has only slowed down European integration and thrown new obstacles in its path.

Labour in Europe must be in the driving seat. The chapters which follow aim to provide a set of political maps. Labour will soon be in power in the UK for the first time in more than seventeen years. We will also be thrust into the heart of a new Europe. When Labour last left office there was no directly elected European Parliament, but no one who was born after 1957 has ever been able to vote for a Labour Government. Now there are dozens of issues crucially affecting Europe on which Labour must take a stance. We have to break with the past to bring about a future of prosperity, independence and peace.

Europe's left must act in the interest of a balanced economic and social future, helping to create jobs and future prosperity, and supporting our vulnerable partners in the Third World, in Central and Eastern Europe and beyond. At every nation-state level, this will require a positive, proactive approach to Europe. A Conservative Government will never make that commitment. Only under a New Labour Government can a new chapter be opened up in Britain's European policy, as we begin to see with Tony Blair the dawning of a new Britain in a new Europe.

ALAN DONNELLY
Economic and Monetary Union

With the publication in May 1995 of the European Commission's Green Paper and in November 1995 of the EMU report on the changeover to the single currency, as well as the final communiqué from the December Madrid Summit on the practical arrangements for its introduction, Economic and Monetary Union returned to the top of Europe's agenda. In the early 1990s EMU seemed doomed as a result of currency speculation and economic turbulence. Yet it is precisely this vulnerability of national currencies which has helped to refocus political support for a single currency in many capitals around Europe.

Stage two of EMU is well under way. The European Monetary Institute has produced its first and second annual reports under the able leadership of Alexander Lamfalussy and the EcoFin Council is pursuing the necessary convergence of inflation, budget deficits and national debt.

The new European Commission remains determined to complete the remaining steps necessary to achieve single currency within the Maastricht Treaty timetable. The Madrid Summit confirmed the blueprint for the final realization of a single currency. The steps to be taken by European institutions, public administrations, the banking and financial sector and enterprises in providing the circumstances which will allow the heads of government to fix exchange rates irrevocably by 1 January 1999, with the first notes appearing by 1 January 2002, have now been set out in detail. The timetable, in three phases, is clear:

A. In the spring of 1998 (as soon as reliable statistical information for 1997 is available), the decision of the Council, meeting at the level of heads of state and government, to launch the single currency.

This is the political signal to banks, enterprises and the public that within a year exchange rates will be irrevocably fixed between participating countries. During 1998, and on the decision of participating countries, the European Central Board will be set up.

B. Followed on 1 January 1999 by the effective beginning of Economic and Monetary Union with the irrevocable fixing of parities and of relevant legislation required for the introduction of the Euro (legal status, continuity of contracts, etc).

During this phase, the scenario envisages a critical mass of financial activities in the single currency built around a single monetary policy emission of new public debt in Euro will be established. These are the two signals that the markets will be waiting for.

C. Completion of the transition – no more than three years later – will see the introduction of notes and coins and the changeover of other payment systems.

This will be the moment when the public start to use the new currency.

The new European Commissioner for Economic and Monetary Affairs, Mr Yves-Thibault de Silguy, clearly intends to proceed with purpose and determination in piloting the final stages of EMU. In the introduction to his 1995 Green Paper on EMU he states, 'By the end of the century, the European Union will have a strong, stable single currency. This is the wish of its people and its leaders in signing and then ratifying the Treaty on European Union.'

He goes on to say, 'When the Treaty was signed, the United Kingdom and Denmark wished to reserve the right not to participate in Monetary Union . . . this opt-out was agreed by the other signatories. This meant that these two member states were able to ratify the treaty, thereby subscribing to all of its provisions – including Protocol 10 by which member states would not *oppose* the transition to a single currency.' This statement is critical, given the predicament of John Major's government. It reminds EU leaders that under the Maastricht Treaty, while they must treat their economic and monetary policy as a matter of common interest within the competent bodies of the Union, those countries outside the first group to join shall not prevent the rest from moving to a single currency. And when that has occurred, those opt-out countries shall not take part in decision-making as far as the actual management of the single currency is concerned.

The Background

The European Community has been attempting to create a single currency for twenty-five years. As the European Monetary System became increasingly dominated by Germany, interest grew in trying to establish an Economic and Monetary Union which would give all participating countries a share in the decision-making rather than being dominated by the Bundesbank. The signing of the Single

European Act and its implementation at the end of 1992 proved to many, particularly those trading across the internal market, that a single currency was an essential part of building an efficient single market.

The lifting of all capital controls to allow free movement of capital within Europe, combined with the free movement of goods and people, led to doubts as to whether these developments were consistent in the long term with the exchange rate mechanism and the operation of entirely separate national monetary policies. The economist T. Padoa-Schioppa warned that (in the long run) the only solution was to complement the internal market with monetary union.

Given the internal market and the increasing influence of the Deutschmark, there has been an increasing worry that, without a single currency, crucial decisions of economic policy in Europe have effectively been transferred to the Bundesbank in Frankfurt. In fairness, the Bundesbank has not sought a mandate to become the unofficial central bank for the European Union. However, some member states have been uneasy about decisions taken by Herr Tietmeyer and his board on the basis of their clear remit to maintain price stability within Germany, because of the consequences these decisions will have on growth and employment in other member states' economies. Therefore, both the Delors report submitted to the Madrid Summit of 1989 (which outlines the 'concrete phases' that would lead to EMU) and the latest Green Paper from Commissioner de Silguy, submitted to the Madrid Summit of 1995, are part of the same process of widening the circle of those involved in taking crucial decisions on economic policy in Europe.

The Benefits

There are a wide range of potential economic benefits to be derived from Economic and Monetary Union. The first key advantage, considering the recent turbulence in currency markets and the negative effects on growth, is the establishment of currency stability and the increased trade that will follow.

- Transaction costs would be substantially reduced as companies and individuals no longer have to transfer between currencies as they make purchases or invest in countries around the European Union. According to the European Commission, such transaction costs amount to 0.5 per cent of the EU's combined GDP. The CBI has estimated that transaction costs across Europe could amount to £10 billion per annum.
- Interest rates could be lower. Exchange rate stability would reduce the risk to investors, enabling governments to lower the risk premium they are required to pay on government securities. Enhanced price stability in some countries, and a better EU average inflation performance would also encourage lower interest rates. The European Commission has estimated that such reduced borrowing costs could increase EU output by up to 2 per cent.
- Internal exchange rate stability would be achieved once and for all, with consequent advantages for investment and improvements in the productive capacity for European industry. Many economists have argued that exchange rate volatility and misalignments have serious long-term costs. For example, the recent Bretton Woods Commission report chaired by Paul Volcker argues that exchange rate volatility since the 1950s and 1960s has been a significant cause of the decline in recent decades of the long-term growth rates of the major

industrialized countries from 5 per cent to 2.5 per cent.
- Speculation against individual European currencies would be eliminated. The risk of a repetition of the currency crisis that threw the pound out of the ERM at a cost of billions in lost foreign exchange reserves would entirely disappear.
- Europe's single currency would become a leading world currency at least as important as the dollar and the yen – increasing the attractions worldwide of trading in a European market-place of nearly 350 million people. It would also help to achieve internal economic policy co-ordination among the big three economic powers, the USA, Japan and Europe.

A single currency could also make it easier for the EU as a whole to achieve and sustain more growth-orientated macroeconomic policies. An expansionary policy, it is argued, cannot be maintained by one country in isolation, but requires EU-wide co-ordination to achieve a lasting increase in output and employment. This 'Euro-Keynesian' argument draws heavily on the ill-fated experience of the French Socialist Government of the early 1980s, which was forced to abandon an expansionary policy that ran counter to the prevailing deflationary trend of its European neighbours. In practice, though, fiscal expansion would require a higher degree of co-ordination than EU countries have yet shown.

The Risks

The benefits of Economic and Monetary Union will, of course, remain theoretical until a single currency has been created and for some the associated loss of monetary independence is a high cost to bear if the advantages made possible by EMU should fail to materialize. For certain European political leaders in government and in opposition, the use of the exchange rate as a tool of economic adjustment and a means of gaining competitiveness is an important mechanism. Europe has recently witnessed a number of exchange-rate adjustments which have effectively acted as competitive devaluation. For countries that are less productive than their trading partners, exchange rate adjustments can boost competitiveness in exports, provided this is not counteracted by higher inflation. Without the ability to adjust the exchange rate, improved competitiveness can only be achieved through complex domestic economic policy which leads to a lower inflation rate than that of other countries. In the past, this has proved difficult to implement and costly to achieve.

In addition to the loss of monetary independence, there are some important problems associated with the Maastricht Treaty. These include the appropriateness of the nominal convergence criteria, the operation of the excessive deficit procedure with its potential deflationary effects, and of course the questions of accountability and transparency of the proposed European Central Bank which, under Maastricht, is designed to be independent from political interference.

Convergence Criteria

It is generally accepted that there will need to be a high degree of convergence among member states of the European Union who intend to participate in EMU. Therefore, convergence criteria are required to establish whether individual member states are able to accept and sustain the single currency. The Maastricht Treaty established four criteria, all nominal monetary or financial indicators. They are set out in Article 109j and in a protocol annexed to the treaty. They require member states to have achieved:

a a high degree of price stability defined as a rate of inflation close to that of the three best-performing states
b sustainable public deficits
c exchange rate stability – by observing the normal fluctuation margins of the ERM
d stable long-term rates – defined as a rate that does not exceed by more than two percentage points that of the three best-performing states.[1]

It is the European Commission's role, using these figures as a guide, to prepare a report on the budgetary policies of member states and express its opinion to EcoFin.

The Council, by majority vote, then determines whether a member state has an excessive deficit and can make recommendations to improve that situation within a certain period of time. If member states ignore the recommendations and show no improvement in their deficit position, the Council can specify exact measures and a timetable for their implementation. The Council can even impose penalties, including the imposition of fines and the obligatory deposit of funds in non-interest-bearing EU accounts.

Article 104c commits the Commission to taking a range of circumstances into consideration when drawing up its report. Perhaps the most flexible provision which the Commission can use in balancing political judgement with simple arithmetic is made in the treaty itself: the Commission must take into account 'whether the government deficit

---

[1] A number of people have suggested alternative convergence criteria, taking proper account of levels of productivity, job creation and growth, and investment. See e.g. Galvin Davies and Martin Brookes.

exceeds government investment expenditures and consider all other relevant factors, including the medium-term economic and budgetary position of the member states.'

While the Bundesbank will continue to press for the most rigorous interpretation of the deficit rules, a flexible interpretation of the procedure should ease the fear of some politicians that national governments would have no scope to allow spending and deficits to rise in the event of an economic downturn, or to maintain their capital investment programmes.

It must be recognized by the political authorities as we move through the final stages of Economic and Monetary Union that the Treaty of European Union has an inherent flexibility which, if applied sensibly, will satisfy the Bundesbank of the seriousness with which member states take the goal of price stability, while at the same time encouraging member states to seek a politically acceptable passage to EMU.

Securing Britain's Interests

The problem for Britain is that EMU has become a taboo subject within John Major's government. Only a week after the publication of the Commission's Green Paper on the implementation of the single currency, Mr Major, hardening his line against EMU, said, 'arguably, the circumstances may not ever be right' for sterling to be merged in a single European currency. The disagreements within his own party are now so deep that his strategy is to assume either that EMU will never happen or, if it does eventually take place, that it will not work. His bottom line, of course, is that since it certainly won't happen until after the next General Election, it should not preoccupy his government.

This approach is hugely damaging to the UK. It not only sends the wrong signals to our partners in Europe, but it also creates uncertainty for our own public authorities, banks and enterprises when they need to know at least that Britain will fully participate in the preparation for the single currency, if not in the final act itself.

Perhaps the most harmful consequence of the Conservatives' ostrich-like approach to a single currency is the effect it has on public opinion about the process and timing of Economic and Monetary Union. By continuing the superficial debate about whether we should be part of a single currency or not, we are missing a much more significant debate, about the practical aspects associated with the introduction of the currency. The EU blueprint calls for a package of measures at the beginning of phase one of the final stage.

The package of measures to be adopted include the following;

1. The legal framework allowing the single currency to be introduced at the start of phase three (1 January 1999). This would include conditions for using the new currency in the different sectors; relations with national currencies; legal status of the Euro; continuity of contracts and legal obligations; and legislation enabling financial and tax authorities to collect some payments in Euro at the start of phase three

2. The characteristics and technical specifications of notes and coins so that cash-handling machines and information systems can be adapted

3. Establishment of a national steering structure for supervising the move to the single currency, involving all the currency users concerned – governments, central bank, private sector and consumers. It would draw up an action

plan for adapting public administration at national and local levels.

4. Perhaps most importantly, definition of a changeover plan in each country by the banking and financial community which would specify the speed and scope of the technical adaptation of its members. Such a plan would establish a number of technical arrangements necessary for a smooth changeover (capital markets and their infrastructures, quotation, settlement, delivery, registration, and wholesale payment systems).

The Commission plan states, 'This package should be prepared in advance and some of the measures should have been adopted, preferably well in advance of the start of phase three of EMU.' The package of measures set out above simply proves that the debate in Britain should focus on these practical questions so that Britain is at least in a position in the spring of 1998 to make a real choice as to whether we want to join the first entry into the single currency. If we do not take these first steps, Britain will not even have the option, because the technical and administrative preparations will not have been made.

Since the end of World War II, we have assumed that we could let the events in the rest of Europe pass us by. This has been our biggest mistake. Time and again, we seem to be surprised when another aspect of European Union is constructed. And having played no role in shaping these developments, we then have to join on someone else's terms.

The most sensible approach for Britain to adopt now would be to recognize that, with a decision at the beginning of 1998 to fix their exchange rates irrevocably within one year, effectively launching Europe's single currency. All the preparation before and during this crucial time must have the complete co-operation of the British government. Should Britain not be seen to be laying this essential groundwork, we would be sending the signal that the UK had no intention of being in the first division of countries joining the single currency. This could pose major risks to Britain's economy and our monetary stability.

It would also have implications for inward investment. Major multinationals taking long-term investment decisions would choose to invest in the Euro zone of the single market rather than in a country that by default could not be in that Euro zone from day one. Furthermore, although the City of London is the financial capital of Europe, the European Central Bank will be in Frankfurt. A failure by the UK at least to make the initial preparations for membership of the single currency would jeopardize the future development of the City of London and would make other financial centres increasingly attractive to investors.

And What of the Single Currency Itself?

Assuming that the British government decides to take all the steps necessary to prepare for entry into a single currency, what considerations should be made in fixing our exchange rates at the beginning of 1999? The most immediate risk for Britain at the time of the decision by the European Council would be whether we could independently resist a severe speculative attack on sterling. This raises the question of whether the UK would require permanently higher interest rates, and whether we would have to live with the fear of a flight of capital investment from the UK.

The timetable for the single currency means there will be a General Election in Britain before the third phase of

EMU. The Shadow Chancellor, Gordon Brown, has successfully established Labour as a potential government concerned with prudent management of our economic and fiscal policy. The medium-term economic strategy outlined by the Shadow Chancellor fits comfortably within the convergence criteria of the Maastricht Treaty. Assuming there is no collapse in Europe's economy during the next three to four years, Britain should be eligible for EMU at the beginning of 1999.

In fact, an incoming Labour Government would find it easier to fulfil its medium-term economic strategy from within the stable Euro zone than from outside it. Britain now needs a constructive policy towards the European Union and an urgent engagement in the process of Economic and Monetary Union.

Once in office, Labour should press for a better balance between economic and monetary co-ordination in Europe. We would negotiate strongly within the context of the Intergovernmental Conference (IGC) for greater economic convergence. We would seek a correct balance between the independent European Central Bank and the elected policymakers in EcoFin and the European Parliament. But only if Britain were engaged positively in the debate about the single currency would we be able to achieve terms acceptable to our national interest. For this reason, the Labour opposition in Westminster should call for Britain to be fully involved *now* in the final technical preparations for the implementation of the single currency.

Public Information and Popular Support

We must recognize that the citizens of Europe need to be properly informed and involved in the very important challenges. Labour needs to press now for an informed debate about the real pros and cons of a single currency. We must support the EU-wide campaign on the benefits of a single currency, including the maintenance of growth and employment across Europe.

The Eurosceptics in Britain have hijacked the government on this matter. The debate is far too important to the future of the United Kingdom to permit small-minded nationalism to have the dominant voice. It is likely that the Conservative Government may even try to turn this into its key campaign issue of the next General Election. Labour must show how important this issue is to the people of Britain and we should stress that it is also a matter of major constitutional significance. Having an independent Central European Bank and reducing parliament's ability to influence monetary policy would be a significant change as would transferring the decision making authority of the external value of our currency to EcoFin. Single currency and a single monetary authority must command wide popular consent and therefore Labour should commit itself to holding a referendum in the United Kingdom on this matter.

Given the timetable outlined by the European Commission, an incoming Labour Government in 1997 should begin implementing the package of technical measures outlined by the Commission for phase three. The government should also play a part in the Council decision to fix parities irrevocably at the beginning of 1999 which will be taken in spring 1996. The period following the Council decision should then be used to negotiate vigorously for the balance of economic and monetary policies outlined earlier in this chapter, to which Labour is already committed. In the autumn of 1998, having negotiated the terms under which Britain would join the single currency, the question of Britain's membership should be put to the people in a public referendum.

None of the major parties in Britain is unequivocally opposed to a single currency. Offering a referendum on the single currency would give those broadly in favour of EMU the opportunity for a proper debate across the nation without being accused of betraying Britain's national interest or of having 'sold out' to Brussels. Of course there are risks involved in holding a referendum. But there are even greater risks in either choosing to stay out of the single currency for fear of a backlash of public opinion, or being accused of élitism by making this fundamental constitutional change without giving the people the right to express their view.

Conclusion

1996 sees Europe's leaders entering the final phase of discussions on the shape of European integration into the twenty-first century. Much will be said on foreign and security policy, particularly in the light of European failure to respond to tragic events in the former Yugoslavia. Consideration will also be given to questions of justice and internal affairs. And of course there will be discussion on how Europe will shape up for the accession of countries from the east.

The great imponderable as we enter this phase is whether the political will or vision exists to embrace this agenda and move Europe to further political integration. While this high drama is played out at summit meeting after summit meeting over the next eighteen months, that other goal of European integration – a single currency – will move into its final and detailed stage of implementation. While there can be little certainty about the conclusions of the 1996

IGC, there is much greater certainty that, by the end of the century, Europe will have its single currency. This will be a formidable achievement for a continent which little more than fifty years earlier had been at war. The choice Britain makes at this time will shape the role we play in Europe for the next fifty years. Let us hope our political leaders at this crucial time will not make the same mistakes made in the 1950s and 1960s. Britain's economic future can only lie at the heart of Europe.

MARK HENDRICK
Employment and Prosperity

Introduction

Our forefathers who fought the Second World War in Europe could never have dreamed that poverty and mass unemployment such as they knew in the thirties might return. In the European Union today, there are already 20 million unemployed, and over 50 million people are living below the poverty line. This is a social tragedy, wasting the skills, talents and hopes of so many people. It also has grave economic consequences, undermining our vitality and competitiveness.

Unemployment undermines the lives of our citizens and their families, and threatens democracy, communities, and social cohesion. It is also expensive – a burden on the taxpayer, the public purse, and the economy. It is, in short, the major economic and social problem confronting the European Union. Failure to combat unemployment will continue to blight the lives of citizens of the EU and could even sow the seeds of another European war.

In Europe, this crisis has occurred not because of, but *despite* the creation of the internal market. The hope that greater economic integration of the member states would help raise the rate of employment has proved short-lived.

Business has prospered and jobs have indeed been created, but not enough. The member states of the EU had an economic growth rate of 3–4% during the second half of the 1980s, creating 10 million jobs in five years, yet unemployment decreased by only 2.8 million people. 'The market' alone is not adequate. It requires the support and guidance of government to create the high skill, high value economy that Europe requires if it is to compete with the rest of the world, and only the left in Europe is prepared to give comprehensive support and guidance.

At the same time, socialists must ask of every policy initiative: does it promote long-term skilled or semi-skilled employment? The renewal of the European economy will entail a capacity to meet new demands from a society where a shrinking minority of human activity will be in agriculture and manufacturing industry. Technology now accounts for the many manual, semi-skilled, and skilled tasks that once provided employment for the masses, and the politicians of the right have abandoned responsibility for an active work-force to the whims of the market. The left must step in with new solutions, providing the work-force with opportunities to secure prosperity.

The information age presents us with new challenges. Our socialist commitments must be retained: social justice and social solidarity, protection for the weak, access for all to health care as required, high standards of education and work, protection for employees, and a structured dialogue between management and labour. Nevertheless, these commitments will need to be adapted to the realities of the twenty-first century.

Addressing social concerns is an investment, not an inconvenience. Employers must be encouraged to gain a broader vision of the role of enterprise in society, and of the important part society can play in enabling enterprise to flourish. They should invest in the young unemployed. They must reassess the importance accorded to shareholding interests, and seek to find a balance between those interests and the work-force stability required to generate the dividend in the first place. They must never forget that business creates and sustains the economic conditions for a stable and productive society.

The Scourge of Unemployment

Unemployment is a 'scourge' which affects us all, whether or not we are out of work ourselves. Technological change over the last thirty years held out the promise of a reduced working week, which would provide more time for leisure, and the possibility of a fairer distribution of work. The 1980s and 1990s so far have shown the reverse to be true, with the creation of what Will Hutton called the 40:30:30 society. In Europe, 40% of adults of working age are in safe jobs, 30% in temporary part-time jobs, and 30% unemployed.[1]

The White Paper 'Growth, Competitiveness, Employment' published by the European Commission under the direction of Jacques Delors identifies three types of unemployment: cyclical, structural and technological. Technological unemployment is essentially a sub-division of structural unemployment; most simply, that part of unemployment which is not reversed by a subsequent upturn in the economic cycle. Structural unemployment arises from the 'gap between the pressures on economies to adapt to change and their ability to do so'.[2] It is this

[1] Will Hutton, *The State We're In*, 1995.
[2] OECD, 1994.

structural unemployment which is hardest to reduce.

The central employment problem faced by European Union countries is the huge component of structural unemployment. In its 'Jobs Study' for 1994, the OECD calculated that the European Union had an unemployment rate for all persons of some 10.6%, compared to 7.2% in North America and 2.5% in Japan. Of that percentage, the structural component is thought to range between 7 and 10% in the European Union countries, while in North America it is estimated at around 6%, and in Japan around 2%. The consequence is that, although Europe is now in recovery, with an expected economic growth of around 3% over the coming two years, unemployment is likely to remain at around 10% for the Union. Recent developments confirm this analysis. Since its peak in spring 1994, unemployment in the EU has come down, but only very slowly. Although growth of GDP in the Union seems to have resumed in mid-1993, this as yet has had minimal impact on the numbers out of work.

Employment indicators

Such underlying statistics are a cause for concern both for the rate of employment, and levels of long-term unemployment, which are the two important employment indicators for comparing Europe's position to our competitors in the United States and Japan.

The employment rate

The employment rate is the ratio of employment to population of working age, and this provides a good measure of the success of economies in providing jobs for their citizens. In 1994, Japan and the US had respective rates of 78% and 70%, in the EU, the employment rate stood at 60%.

This low rate is partly accounted for by the diminishment of the labour force between 1990 and 1994. The 'lack of job opportunities seems to have persuaded a significant proportion of men in particular either to withdraw from the labour force or to delay entry'.[3] The most disturbing aspect of this development is the significant number of men aged between 25 and 54 who withdrew from the formal labour market. This trend was particularly marked in Italy, Ireland, and the UK and, in total, was responsible for reducing the EU's work-force by almost 1.2 million over that four-year period.

This suggests there is a hidden pool of unemployment: people who are not at present accounted for in official counts as they are not actively seeking employment, people who are part of the black market, or who are not eligible for work. This could amount to as many as 4.8 million people. When these, the disenfranchized unemployed, are encouraged by a favourable economic situation to re-enter the job market, the jobless figures will clearly not come down. More importantly, this hidden 20% represents a further waste of the economic potential and productive capacity of the EU.

Long-term unemployment

When employment increased in the late 1980s, the demand for labour focused on new and flexible skills. Many of those already unemployed were thus equipped to compete effectively. The result is that, of the 10.6% unemployment we have in Europe today, a staggering proportion – over 40% – is composed of the long-term unemployed (persons unemployed continuously for one year and more). This is more severe than in North America and Japan, where long-

---

[3] 'Employment in Europe', 1995

term unemployment as a proportion of the total unemployed stands at only 11.2% and 15.4% respectively.

The plight of the 'never employed' – who haven't worked since leaving school – and the long-term unemployed is different from, and far worse than that of the short-term unemployed. A marginalized underclass is forming, increasingly alienated from accepted forms of civic participation, bitter and excluded, becoming less employable, disillusioned with trying to be employable, and often locked inexorably by absurd social policies into unemployment.

Employers are neither keen to fill their vacancies with the long-term unemployed nor willing to engage in long-term retraining. The long-term unemployed are effectively removed from the job market. It is therefore possible for employers to experience labour and skills shortages even though there are millions of long-term unemployed. Labour-market policies in favour of the short-term unemployed may quite plausibly fuel wage inflation, because the millions of long-term unemployed crying out for a job lack the requisite skills.

Employment Patterns and Job Losses

Global trends

It is important to analyse where job losses have occurred, where jobs are being created, and to identify the industrial sectors where the member states of the Union have the capacity to compete, in order to establish the skills relevant to the industries of the future. Among OECD countries, the trends are as follows.

Agriculture is a sector which is rapidly decreasing in size. In 1994 it amounted to only 7% of OECD civilian employment, compared with 14% in 1970. The importance of employment in manufacturing industry has also decreased, down from almost 40% of OECD employment in 1970 to 30% in 1992.

It is in the service sector that employment has been created, rising from 50% of OECD employment in 1970 to 65% in 1992. These trends are likely to continue, and should be encouraged where appropriate. Service provision is no longer in competition with, but supplements and even stimulates, the production of goods. For example, the introduction of information services has stimulated the sale of information technology. Services are now an integral part of production and often make use of high-technology goods with a high added value. They are therefore good for the economy as a whole.

The 'greying' of Europe

The demographic development of the European Union points to a significant and increasing demand for services. The European population will soon cease to grow, largely because of a dramatic fall in birth rates. There are 348 million people today in the EU, and this figure is expected to increase slightly up to the year 2005, but then a gentle decline is anticipated. In the year 2020 the population should be no higher than it is today.

In its report, 'The Demographic Situation of the European Union', the European Commission estimates that the number of children and young people will decrease by 9 million up to the year 2020. The active generation, those who are expected to work and produce to ensure our prosperity, will decrease by 9 million people over the same period. However, the retired population will grow by 18 million people. This is an increase of 35%, from 52 to 70 million people. Europe will require a highly skilled, highly productive work-force, working in a high-tech environment, if sufficient wealth is to be generated to satisfy the needs of both those with work, and those without it – which includes those in retirement. It will need an increase of almost 50% across the board in productivity just to stand still.

International trade
The White Paper 'Growth, Competitiveness, Employment' asked the question 'where is growth?' Whereas between 1988 and 1990, three quarters of world output came from OECD countries and only one quarter from developing countries, it is estimated that from 1989 to the year 2000, less than two-thirds of world output will come from OECD countries, and more than one third from developing countries. This globalization of the economy presents a huge opportunity for the Union, alongside the shift in emphasis towards a highly skilled services sector. As the OECD notes, 'imports from non-OECD countries are in substantial part labour-intensive manufactured products and primary materials, whereas exports by OECD countries very often have a relatively high skill content'.[4]

The report also indicates that although there does appear to have been a slight negative effect on demand for unskilled labour in OECD countries due to trade with non-OECD countries, losses of unskilled jobs have been largely offset by jobs gained through exports of goods and services produced by skilled labour.

The message is clear. The way forward economically, for the UK and the EU, is to create a highly skilled workforce, increase our investment capacity, and promote new and appropriate technologies and services which will be

[4] OECD, 'Jobs Study', 1994.

the key to successful competition in the modern global economy.

The Challenge of Unemployment

The European approach
Jacques Delors demanded that Europe be more than just a market-place. The objective of the EU is 'to promote throughout the community a harmonious and balanced development of economic activities, sustainable and non-inflationary growth respecting the environment, a high degree of convergence of economic performance, a high level of employment and social protection'.[5] This is not just an approach to the unemployment question, it is the guiding principle for the creation of a European Community.

Alongside the economic dimension which European integration brings, there must be a social dimension. Europe must be more than just a free trade area, or a 'common market'. It must be a community with the degree of economic, social and political integration and cohesion which reflects the aims and aspirations of its people. This is fundamental to the Labour Party's position on Europe.

The economic integration of Europe, spurred towards completion by the single market, has raised a wide range of social issues. The single market has certainly brought growth for the UK since 1992. For example, nearly £17 billion was invested in the UK by firms from within the European Union during this period. According to the OECD, EU firms now provide over 150,000 jobs in the manufacturing sector alone. Even in the car sector, in which

---

[5] Article 2 of the Treaty of the European Community.

the Japanese have made such an important contribution to the UK, OECD statistics show that 67% of all new jobs in the industry between 1985–90 were created by European investment.

Yet the single market must be complemented by social policy. First, because a dynamic social policy is inseparable from an efficient industrial policy, and second, because market forces tend towards a concentration of capital and growth in the better-off areas and sections of the EU population – to the detriment of those who enter the 'level playing-field' with a structural or geographic handicap.

Vocational training for workers and the improvement of the occupational and geographical mobility of labour, for example, are prerequisites for the efficiency of European industry. Likewise, Community aid granted to workers who have to abandon such trades as textiles and agriculture to retrain makes it easier to absorb economic change. There is no trade-off between the economic and the social; the two must go hand-in-hand.

The Commission's White Paper on 'Growth, Competitiveness, Employment' seeks to analyse the problems of unemployment at the global level, in terms of competitiveness, and at a more local level, in terms of job creation. But the central novelty of the White Paper is not so much in the content of individual policy initiatives as political: the aim is to give a clear priority to employment creation in the Union. It does this by setting an explicit target for the reduction of unemployment – to create 15 million jobs by the year 2000 – and by seeking to organize the whole range of European Union policies around this objective. Above all, the White Paper affirms the need to find the right mix of policies to promote growth and competitiveness and at the same time guarantee social protection and solidarity.

The policy initiatives stemming from this objective can be divided into two types: on the one hand, measures aimed at increasing the demand for labour by improving industrial performance; and, on the other, measures aimed at labour-market reform and a better match between labour supply and demand. The first type covers an enormous range of areas, from investment in research and technological development to competition policy. The second type involves measures aimed at labour-market reform, to achieve a better adaptation of labour supply to demand. It is here that conflict with the right – and the British Conservative Government in particular – has been most fierce. In this area, all the essential powers are held (and are likely to remain) at national level. The EU's role is merely to address common problems and to cajole member states towards common solutions.

Facilitating employment creation
Europe's Structural Funds, which are a source of additional investment, should and must bring added value to national initiatives.

One such Structural Fund is the European Social Fund (ESF) for training and retraining, whose priority is to help the unemployed. Objective 3 covers measures to combat long-term unemployment and to promote the vocational integration of young persons into the labour market. Objective 4 seeks to prevent job losses by allowing companies, by means of a subsidy, to retain and retrain workers in companies under threat. This is similar to the Japanese government's scheme to help industrial sectors in crisis. Yet the British Conservative Government has stated that it will take no part in projects under Objective 4. These, it says, should be done away with, in favour of Objective 3 priorities.

The Labour Party supports Objective 4 measures as the sensible, long-term approach, and as an important weapon to be added to Europe's arsenal in the battle against unemployment. It is the approach of every other member state within the EU. The Labour Party also believes that economic success can only be achieved through close co-ordination of economic policies between EU member states to promote investment, create jobs and boost growth.[6]

Co-ordination

Co-ordination of policies and instruments between member states involves analysing the overall employment systems (including, for example, the interplay of taxation and social policies), with the aim of improving employment generation. Though all the key economic decisions affecting employment continue to be made at national level, the EU is nonetheless developing a mandate to advise and to set guidelines outside which it would be politically difficult for member states to operate.

In December 1994 the framework for a concerted attack on unemployment was set by the European Council's Essen Agreement. This broke new ground in committing each of the member states to set out a multi-annual employment programme, to be monitored by both the Council of Ministers and the Commission. These multi-annual programmes are to focus on five key proposals:

1. Improving employment opportunities by promoting investment in vocational training, for example, through the EU's Socrates Programme.

2. Increasing the employment intensiveness of growth, in

---

[6] The future of the European Union: Report on Labour's Position for the IGC 1996.

particular through the promotion of job-creating initiatives at regional and local level.

3. Reducing non-wage labour costs extensively enough to ensure that there is an incentive for the hiring of employees.

4. Improving the system of getting people into work, whether through active labour market measures or through positive use of social protection and income support.

5. Improving measures to help social groups which are particularly hard hit by unemployment; for example, ethnic minorities.

The Essen Agreement formed a good basis on which to work. The Essen proposals are general, and leave scope for member states to carry them out in a manner they consider to be politically acceptable.

The macroeconomic environment

A stable macroeconomic framework will provide the base for effective structural reforms. The ultimate aim should be a path of higher growth, lower unemployment, an improved fiscal position, and increased competitiveness. These are carefully balanced priorities for a Labour Government, which would enable the UK to make its contribution to reducing EU unemployment.

If the UK is to have influence in the important economic and monetary decisions to be made in the future, it is essential that it retains the option to move towards a single currency in 1999. This option would be dependent upon the UK meeting the Maastricht convergence criteria for monetary union, and also, two other important considerations.

First of all, 'real' economic considerations should be taken into account, such as GDP growth rates, competitivity and employment levels, and not just the Maastricht 'nominal' criteria of debt and deficit ratios and inflation. Without real convergence between member states, there will be economic 'shocks' across a single currency area, which could do the UK's economy more harm than good. Monetary union between East and West Germany highlighted this problem. Therefore, the 1996 intergovernmental conference must revise the treaty on which the EU is founded, placing stronger emphasis on employment generation as part of the preparation for monetary union.

Secondly, monetary union requires consent. It requires the trust of the people, the businesses, and the institutions that will use the new currency.

The employment consequences of EMU are difficult to predict. EMU is merely a framework within which a whole range of policy directions could be taken. The predictions of some economists that even more unemployment might result from EMU are pessimistic. The European Parliament's report 'A Coherent Employment Strategy for the European Union' suggests in its explanatory statement that up to 10 million jobs could be lost if all member states meet the Maastricht deficit and debt requirements within five years, based on a study carried out by the NIESR in London.[7] This scenario is unrealistic, because several member states do not expect to meet the criteria for entry in 1999. In any case, the argument is unlikely to apply to the UK, which is already close to meeting the convergence criteria.

---

[7] 'The Coates Report':A Coherent Employment Strategy for the European Union, 1995.

The consequences of the UK not going ahead with a single currency must be considered. There would almost certainly be a run on the pound as investors flocked to the more stable single currency. At the same time, inward investment from countries such as the US and Japan would begin to 'dry up'. Investors currently favour the UK because it gives them access to the European single market while enabling them to conduct business in English. If the UK chose not to play a full part in the economic integration and decision-making of Europe, new investors would opt to locate their businesses in mainland Europe. This in turn would cost jobs and do more damage to employment in the UK than the Maastricht convergence criteria ever could.

A Programme to Deal with Unemployment

Action on people

The rise in employment at the end of the eighties led to a demand for a work-force with new and flexible skills. Many of those already unemployed were not equipped to compete effectively. The new jobs therefore went to young people and women returners with the required skills. Unemployment thus becomes a permanent state, preserved by a fundamental mismatch between skills and needs. It is not a recruitment reserve – it is a splitting of society into those likely and those never likely to find work.

The OECD has pointed out that people now entering work can expect six or more changes in a working life. Part of education will therefore have to take the form of 'learning how to learn' throughout our working lives. It is clear from the analysis of future growth areas that the emphasis on skills is only likely to increase. Ensuring good levels of skills is vital if, as individuals, people are to enter the job market on a competitive basis. It is also vital to a cohesive and prosperous society. The failure to ensure effective re-skilling is creating a two-speed labour market, and this has three extremely negative effects: first, it means an increase in long-term unemployment as turnover in jobs involves the same band of people; second, it causes problems for expanding firms unable to find the skilled labour they require; third, this leads to slower growth and continuing pressure on public finances.

In 'What's Working (and what's not)', Robert Reich, the US Secretary of Labour, identifies re-skilling as the key area for job creation and preservation: 'creating a culture of lifelong learning, and constructing an institutional structure to give force to that culture, are the core strategies for improving the incomes of ordinary working Americans.' The point applies equally to Europe.

Action on people is therefore fundamental to any meaningful response by governments. And it is particularly fundamental in the UK, which now has a lower proportion of young people participating in higher education than new industrial competitors such as South Korea and Taiwan. The World Economic Forum has relegated Britain in its table of the availability of skills in the OECD countries: out of twenty-two countries, we are now nineteenth, behind both Ireland and Turkey.

The promotion of on-the-job training for adults is a prime area for trade union action, and it is a priority to which trade unions accord increasing importance. The suggestion by the TUC, for example, that by 2000 all employees should take part in at least five days' training and development activities each year is an extremely good one. Devising a scheme which encourages firms to invest in their work-force is vital. At present, many employers, concerned with profit maximization objectives, simply dismiss workers with obsolete skills and hire others who already have the requisite skills.

A system which requires a contribution by both employers and employees towards a compulsory number of days' training per year needs to be evolved. The Labour Party's call for a revision of accountancy standards, so as to attribute adequate asset value to investments in intangibles such as R&D and skills, is another positive step. This should encourage investors to invest in firms with proven track records in training their work-forces.

Active Labour Market Policies

Currently, 2–3% of GDP in European Union countries is spent on labour-market policies. Of this, the OECD has calculated that less than 1% is allocated to active measures. This is inadequate, and reform is required to achieve a better balance between passive income support on the one hand, and measures which improve access to the labour market and jobs, develop job-related skills, and promote more efficient labour markets on the other.

In any revision of the present system, reform must aim to involve the key actors at local level – employers, trade unions, educational institutions and local government – in a combined effort to develop programmes that respond to local needs.

Active measures are required to help the long-term unemployed in particular. Countries where employment benefits are available for longer periods have higher rates of long-term unemployment. But the American approach, of reducing the duration of benefit availability, with no back-up support, is not the answer. One possible solution would be for the state to guarantee to find work for the unemployed after one year, and to pay six months' benefit to which the unemployed individual would have otherwise been entitled to the employer directly. This approach would keep people active and productive, while giving them the opportunity to gain experience.

Competitiveness and entrepreneurship

The EU is heavily involved in the promotion of entrepreneurship, which is rightly seen as a key to competitiveness. In a world where the most competitive firms are those best equipped to adapt and respond to change, an entrepreneurial spirit is what enables a company to keep one step ahead of the rest. Good government can remove the red tape, regulations and controls that discourage new and expanding enterprises. It can also help promote the type of economic unit now recognized as best able to respond rapidly in the face of new challenges – the forward-looking small and medium-sized enterprise (SME) with fewer than 500 workers.

Companies, and in particular these forward-looking SMEs, are becoming competitive by improving productivity per worker. They are adopting efficient management practices, introducing new technologies and working methods. According to the European Commission, SMEs employed 70% of the European work-force in 1994. In 1990 there were 16.4 million SMEs in the EU. Evidence of their competitiveness abounds.

The competitiveness of SMEs makes them an essential instrument for job creation within the European Union. Compared to both the US and Japan, the EU has had a poor record of job creation in the private sector over the last twenty years: according to the OECD, some two-thirds of the ten million jobs created in the EU and EFTA since the early 1970s have been in the public sector. Job creation in the private sector is clearly an area where much can be done, and it is a challenge which socialists must take up whole-heartedly. This can only be achieved by co-operation between the public sector and the private sector.

The Commission's recognition of the importance of SMEs is extremely encouraging. Its contribution takes two forms. First, it is re-examining the legal and fiscal environment to ensure it does not act as a brake on business development. Second, it provides direct support to SMEs through measures financed by the Structural Funds. The Business and Innovation Centres (BICs) are a good example of the way the Commission works in this area. These are set up by the Commission with public and private partners. They provide a comprehensive programme of services (training, finance, marketing, technology transfer and more) to SMEs which are developing innovatory technology-based projects.

An enormous range of action is being taken at Community level to promote SMEs. At the same time, it is important to ensure that use of public funds is carefully controlled – and in particular that Community funding is used as a complement to, and not a replacement for, national schemes and spending. This is the principle of 'additionality', and it is the basis on which the EU supports schemes. A Labour Government must ensure that this effort continues, both in Europe and at home. Its long-term goal must be to foster entrepreneurship in a decentralized economy.

Flexible Working-time

Flexible working-time does not offer a permanent solution to the unemployment problem. However, it ensures labour-market flexibility, so that supply can better meet demand, while meeting employees' needs for greater freedom to organize their own time. Flexibility is best achieved by employers co-operating with workers' representatives to find the best solution for their particular enterprise.

An excellent example of this took place at Volkswagen, in Germany. The company found itself forced to reduce its work-force by 30% because of a massive drop in demand. Instead of mass redundancies, a reduction and redistribution of working-time was successfully negotiated with employees. Individual employees now work shorter hours and earn a lower wage, but redundancies were avoided. By such means, companies can maintain a skills pool, even though skills may be temporarily under-employed.

The trend towards a service economy, the growth of a female labour force and the new technologies, with their opportunities for teleworking, are rendering the old model of work organization obsolete. Governments must ensure that the regulatory framework allows for more flexibility, and that the taxation regime positively encourages it.

Employment Trends

The inaction of the British Conservative Government is causing Britain to fall behind, handicapped by investment gaps and skills shortages, while research and development spending is low and badly targeted. The result is that growth in Britain is now slower than in any comparable period since the Second World War. Our trend growth rate, as estimated by the OECD, is slower than any of the other G7 countries.

Furthermore, though unemployment has fallen in the UK to 8.7%, this official figure must be qualified. First, compared to our European partners, the UK requirements for unemployment benefit plus massaging of the statistics gives a false picture. Second, the number of long-term unemployed has actually risen, currently representing 37% of the unemployed, against 34% at the end of 1992. Third, the majority of new jobs which have been created have tended to be part-time and generally in low-skill areas. Between 1990 and 1994, more than 500,000 people moved into part-time work. On the other hand, full-time jobs keep falling despite the recovery, and in numbers that outweigh any new jobs created.

In principle, an increase in part-time employment presents no particular problem, but the danger in the UK is that much part-time work is low-paid, unskilled and offers no guaranteed social protection. It may seem better to have some work than none at all, but the emergence of a raft of second-class jobs is not a good recipe for the future. According to the Joseph Rowntree Association, income inequality in the UK grew rapidly between 1977 and 1990, reaching its highest post-war level.

There is, therefore, both a human and an economic cost to the Conservative Government's approach. Despite the rhetoric about high skills and high technology, the reality is that they have produced a low skill, low-cost economy. This strategy is flawed. All the evidence shows that only a high-skill economy is a viable option for UK competitiveness.

An analysis published in the *New York Times* (6 August, 1993) evaluated the hourly cost to employers per industrial worker, including wages, benefits and taxes. Germany had labour costs of US$26.90 per hour; the US, $15.89 per hour; Spain, $14.70 per hour; and the UK rate was $14.61 per hour. By OECD standards, this put the UK in a low bracket. Yet labour costs in Taiwan and South Korea stand at $5.19 and $4.93 per hour respectively. This differential is clearly too great for significant employment gains to be made in Europe from wage reductions. A low-wage economy is a no-win economic strategy, which is detrimental to our industrial capacity and pointless in terms of our competitiveness.

A number of pressing issues confront the Labour Party in taking action on jobs. Switching the non-wage element of labour costs to other forms of taxation needs very careful examination. It is a sensitive area for the left, but must be tackled. Finding a system to deal with the poverty trap is another difficult area: a balance must be sought which makes it profitable to work, while providing protection for those unable to work.

A realistic minimum wage is a priority for the Labour Party which must be implemented. Since the abolition of the wages councils in August 1993, Britain has become the only country in Europe without legal pay protection for the poorest. Such protection, when set at a realistic level, contributes to social justice and economic success. It raises skills and reduces labour turnover rates.

Regulation versus Deregulation

In 1989 the member states of the European Union adopted the EU's Social Charter, underpinning the belief that the development of a large European labour market should improve the living and working conditions of workers in the Community. The fundamental rights enshrined in the Social Charter are: freedom of movement, employment and fair pay; the improvement of living and working conditions; social protection; freedom of association and of collective bargaining; vocational training; equal treatment for men and women; availability of information; consultation and participation of workers; the protection of health and safety in the workplace; and the protection of children and adolescents, the elderly and the disabled.

The Social Charter laid down principles, and in order for these to be put into practice, directives establishing minimum standards for Europe had to be unanimously adopted by the Council. They were continually 'watered down' to try to satisfy the UK Conservative Government, but this government ensured that effective directives were systematically blocked, and to break this deadlock the Social Protocol was signed at Maastricht, authorizing the other member states to give effect to directives under the Social Charter without the involvement of the UK.

This opt-out excludes Britain from any involvement in setting the agenda for European social policy. Britain is thus barred from discussing legislation which will affect British companies operating in European markets. It also threatens to lead to social 'dumping' in the UK, undermining standards in the rest of the Community, and further eroding the quality of everyday life in Britain. It is a central plank of Labour's manifesto to strengthen and sign the Social Charter.

The main item adopted under the Social Protocol procedures, but not applied to Britain, is the European Works Council. This directive was designed to enable European employees of multinational companies to be informed and consulted about what goes on inside these massive corporations when large-scale redundancies, restructuring, mergers, corporate reorganization, or the introduction of product or process innovations and work practices occur.

The directive provides for the establishment, either on the initiative of the company or group management or at the written request of at least 100 employees or their representatives in at least two member states, of a 'special negotiating body', to exchange constructive proposals from both sides.

This is no dramatic development, merely the establishment of a framework within which employers and workers' representatives are encouraged to negotiate. Yet the directive has been controversial because the issues raised by the debate on information and consultation go to the heart of the central question for social policy, namely, what type of European social model will help European industry to become more competitive?

On one side are those, generally from the right, who call for deregulation: job protection legislation and collective agreements have, they say, made many firms think twice before hiring extra labour because of the difficulties and costs of subsequent redundancies. Unions, they say, further aggravate the impact on employment by defending the interests of those in work above other concerns. There may be a grain of truth in some of these arguments, but the type of regulation which is currently being promoted at European level is of quite a different kind. These are regulations which recognize the need for a decentralized approach, and which focus on providing a framework for industry which promotes high levels of skills and productivity.

The crude dichotomy of deregulation versus regulation is not helpful. The emphasis should be placed instead on a co-operative approach within industry, a partnership between work-force and employers which should be of mutual benefit. This is the best way to promote competitiveness. It is precisely this type of partnership which the Works Council directive is seeking to promote at European level. Despite the British 'opt-out' on this directive, several large

UK companies are establishing their own voluntary agreements on information and consultation.

Conclusions

What will be the tasks of a Labour Government in Europe? A Labour Government will have to undo more than sixteen years of damage inflicted by the Conservative Government on the UK. The priority of a Labour Government will be to get people back to work. We must also monitor important economic indicators which will determine Britain's involvement in a single currency and manage the nation's economy sensibly. This is essential if there is to be sustainable and non-inflationary growth in the economy. It is also essential if the UK is to exercise the option of moving to join a European single currency when the time is right.

Unemployment is not just a UK problem. It is a pan-European issue that must be tackled by member states co-ordinating their individual economic policies. The Delors White Paper forms the basis of a concerted programme of action to reduce unemployment by 15 million by the year 2000. However, this political aim needs the practical back-up of member states if it is not to become merely idealistic rhetoric. The European Parliament and Commission and financial institutions can assist with the direction and co-ordination of the White Paper, and the EU Structural Funds will also help to create jobs. However, it is the responsibility of national government, national institutions and businesses to provide the majority of the resources required, if unemployment is to be dealt with effectively. Member states' governments must act together in order to achieve the aims of the Delors White Paper. We need the resources to back the principles and governments could do much more to support this initiative.

An effective programme to put the nation back to work needs investment in people, to enable them to develop the requisite skills for the economy of the twenty-first century. This means high-quality education and training. It needs active labour-market policies which encourage job creation in areas which meet the needs of the 'information age'. It needs action on jobs, and intervention so that partnership between the public sector and the private sector can enable the economy to flourish, and provide prosperity for all citizens. An employment programme must tap the competitive and entrepreneurial skills of all of our people, so that everyone can play their part in shaping the new Europe and in building a country that is prosperous and proud.[8]

---

[8] I would like to thank Gwilym Jones for helping with the research for this chapter.

ERYL McNALLY
European Union Research and Development

Over one and a half million people within the European Union are directly employed in Research and Development (R&D) – about one per cent of the total labour force. Half of these are the technologists and scientists who spearhead essential technological research. In 1994 the expenditure on this research was equivalent to some 100 billion ecu (75p a day for each of us). Yet we are not keeping pace in trade, especially in high-technology goods, with our trading partners, Japan and the USA. There is insufficient and inefficient R&D, a problem highlighted in the 1994 Delors White Paper on Growth, Competitiveness and Employment. This White Paper gave figures of 2% of GDP for R&D expenditure in the EU compared to 2.4% in the USA and 2.8% in Japan. Within the EU, there is considerable geographical variation, with a lower proportion of expenditure in poorer countries and regions. This is less true in Japan and the US.

There is a Luddite way of looking at the world biased against R&D: taking the view that jobs are lost with technological advance. These have to be replaced by new and different jobs which rarely match the skill mix and the geographical location of those destroyed. The current problem of unemployment largely occurs because of the global nature of trade, with world-wide markets and competition from what are increasingly low-wage and high-skilled economies. The EU can remain amongst the most prosperous areas in the world only by keeping ahead of the high-technology game with labour productivity multiplied by a constantly updated infrastructure. Highly paid and highly profitable workers can be employed and will underpin service sectors of the economy, although even here technology creates a global market.

Technological development under democratic control will benefit our society. In certain fields ethical and moral considerations must have their sway. In biotechnology, for example, rules are needed to limit what bio-manipulation is acceptable. These rules may cause chagrin to various sections of the biotechnology industry. It is necessary to have a political overview of R&D to direct and channel developments towards job creation rather than reducing skills in the workplace, empowering rather than destroying the work-force, protecting the environment rather than placing harsh demands on it. Politicians must be pro-active and ensure training and investment in new areas of work such as informatics and biotechnology before massive technology-induced redundancies occur. But the wrong kind of R&D would be equally disastrous. Europe needs appropriate R&D. The EU has failed this test in the past.

Who spends it?

The majority of R&D expenditure within Europe (63%) is by businesses such as General Motors, Glaxo Welcome and Hitachi, of which the majority (80%) is self-financed; only 20% coming from individual governments or the EU. As this list suggests, many are international companies controlled from outside the EU. A further 18% is spent by universities whilst the remainder is spent by other agencies such as member states themselves and European research centres such as ESA (European Space Agency). Governments account for just under 50% of all R&D expenditure Europe-wide, via grants to universities, businesses and research centres and via the EU.

Direct EU expenditure upon R&D, indirectly paid for by member states, amounted to only 3% of the total European R&D effort in 1994 and this needs to be borne in mind when the EU is expected simultaneously to solve the problems of competiveness and employment. It is a miserly amount compared with EU spending upon the CAP (Common Agricultural Policy) which takes 53% of EU spending, while the Structural Funds take 32%, far outstripping the 3.6% spent upon R&D. Priorities must change, with significant reductions in the CAP and increases in R&D. A British Labour Government should have no difficulty here. Within the R&D Budget, Britain gets back more than it contributes.

A sectoral analysis of British Government R&D spending shows that military R&D expenditure accounts for about 25%, followed closely by the university sector and then the non-military industrial sector which accounts for about 13%. This overemphasizes the defence sector and there is considerable evidence that this has contributed to the post-war decline of the UK compared to Japan. The argument that military R&D benefits industry is now suspect. Increasingly, new military hardware does not even contain state-of-the-art civilian technologies. It is over-elaborate and over-engineered; the final manifestation of Victorian electro-mechanical technologies. The sums spent on defence R&D exceed the combined (non-military) R&D budgets of the EU and all other Europe-wide research organizations. However this defence R&D is heavily biased towards just two member states, the UK and France. It is a significant amount, not only in cash terms, but also because of its cost to society by sterilizing the work of tens of thousands of qualified scientists and engineers. We need to cash in the peace dividend, with the resources thus released being diverted into the fight to improve competitiveness. In France and the UK, where 40% or more of government R&D spending is on defence, this will be particularly crucial. Jacques Chirac's antics in the Pacific don't augur well. At the EU level there is a need for more programmes (such as the arms conversion programme KONVER) to aid conversion from military industries to civil industries. There is a clear role here for a European version of Labour's proposed Defence Diversification Agency.

Not all Europe-wide R&D is EU-funded. Significant work is carried out by other co-operative European facilities and agencies such as the well-known CERN (European Centre for Nuclear Research). Overall, the combined cost of these non-EU ventures is currently nearly 6 billion ecu, about 6% of Europe's R&D effort and almost twice that spent by the EU.

CERN is a good example of these Europe-wide agencies. It was established in 1954 by international treaty with the remit to research into high-energy particle physics and is now an internationally respected laboratory that straddles the border of France and Switzerland with its enormous particle accelerator. While such co-operation is necessary, since it would be impossibly costly for a single nation state to underwrite the costs involved, there is nevertheless increasing pressure for such research to have clear industrial applications.

In all, there are 10 non-EU European-wide centres:

- European Organization for Nuclear Research
- European Microbiological laboratory

- European Space Agency
- European Southern Observatory
- EUREKA
- European Co-operation in Scientific and Technical Research
- European Molecular Biology Organization
- European Synchroton Radiation Facility
- Institute Max von Laue-Paul Langevin
- European Science Foundation

Most of these bodies have membership beyond the European Union, in Switzerland, Norway and sometimes Eastern European States as well as co-operative arrangements further afield. However, some of these organizations initially grew from a lack of an EU R&D commitment. Now their continued role should be reviewed within the context of an expanded EU effort.

One particular example of intergovernmental co-operation not based upon a central laboratory is the EUREKA programme, started in 1985 as Europe's answer to Star Wars. Its general objectives are 'to increase European productivity and competitiveness through closer co-operation between firms and research institutes in advanced technologies, developing products, processes and services with a world market potential'. It has had, it is claimed, about 14 billion ecu of funding, including 1.3 billion ecu in 1994. Viewed favourably, this is a diverse series of consortia-based projects ranging from just a few partners to many hundreds. But it can increasingly be seen as a clever PR packaging of projects that would have been carried out in any case, a nameplate R&D programme. The partnerships, which must be cross-national, come from both universities and businesses that have achieved EUREKA status. Each country has its own national project co-ordinator and its own rules for administering the applications. An annual ministerial conference gives overall guidance and accepts new projects with advice from representatives from each of the participating countries.

The organization COST (Co-operation in the field of Scientific and Technical Research), which was set up in 1971 and had 400 million ecu funding in 1994, is a third parallel system. Some rationalization is obviously needed. EU R&D spending should have EUREKA aims and not be hamstrung by competition rules designed for the era of nation-state technology in the global marketplace.

The Role of the European Union

The European Union's Research and Development programmes started with research for the European Steel and Coal Community, to which nuclear research was added and then more general research. In the 1992 Maastricht Treaty, the emphasis of EU R&D was quite clearly redirected towards industrial competitiveness, with two additional objectives of, firstly, co-ordination between EU and member states' R&D and, secondly, R&D for any other area in which the EU has competence, such as the environment. This triple objective is supposedly implemented through the multi-annual 'Framework' programmes that gather the various strands of Research and Development activities into a cohesive whole. A Framework Programme is put forward in considerable detail by the Commission and then unanimous agreement sought within the Council of Ministers for the overall content, budget and direction.

As yet, little has changed. The European Parliament has been given important co-decision powers for these Framework Programmes and also has to be consulted on the detail of the specific programmes. If we are to effect the shift away from the burden of past R&D programmes, it is necessary that the unanimity principle currently in force within the Council of Ministers be replaced with qualified majority voting to prevent special interests who want to block change from damaging the whole EU R&D programme. Equally, there needs to be more transparency on what takes place within the Council. Currently, governments hide hard decisions beneath the cloak of collective responsibility.

The specific programmes
Currently, the Union is completing the Third Framework programme, has started on the Fourth Framework and is now preparing the Fifth Framework for implementation from 1998 so that there can be a seamless transition every four years without having to put researchers in limbo between programmes.

The Fourth Framework programme has a vast number of projects but these specific programmes are gathered together into groups to give an overview of the contents.[1] The largest proportion of money is for information and

---

[1] The nineteen specific programmes within the Framework Programme are: information technology, telematics, communications technologies, industrial and materials technologies; standards, measurement and testing; environment and climate; marine science and technology; biotechnology; biomedicine and health; agro-industrial research; clean and efficient energy technologies; nuclear fission safety; controlled thermonuclear fusion; transport; socio-economics; co-operation with third-world countries and international organizations; dissemination and exploitation of research results; training and mobility of researchers; Joint Research Centre. This list is too long for the present budget to withstand.

Each of the specific programmes is subdivided and further divided into particular project areas that are put out to tender. Universities, large businesses, some SMEs and specialist laboratories keep a close eye out

communication technologies where the needs of users are now thankfully being addressed above those of the technologies. The 'information super-highway' is strongly represented, including multimedia and such projects for telemedicine services as heart monitoring and remote consultation. Industrial and materials technologies take up 16% of the resources, life sciences 12% and the environment just under 9%. All are intended to be programmes that co-ordinate and enhance national efforts whilst reducing duplication.

Programmes which are significant for renewable energy and for energy efficiency – the ALTENER, JOULE and THERMIE programmes – are of benefit not only to the EU but also world-wide. The EU commitment to reduce carbon dioxide levels, initially to their 1990 values and then much further can only be implemented by utilizing the R&D from these programmes. The European Parliament is particularly keen to see their translation into commercial reality. It takes time to implement commercially viable research results and it is only the carrot and stick approach of the EU that is gradually dragging industry into this area. Bio-mass and wind-power are perhaps the two best-known examples, but there are many hundreds of other

---

for these opportunities and form partnerships which are required to be both multinational and include an SME partner to bid for a project. Each bid has to come with matching funding as the EU pays a maximum of 50% of the cost of the research. In practice, there is a degree of autonomy available to well-developed partnerships to suggest projects within the broad specification laid down by the Commission. The selection process is performed essentially by subject experts from both within and outside the Commission. This works well at choosing within the fields, but poorly at weeding out fields in technological decline and is liable to be biased by Commission officials massaging expert views to fit their own research predictions. An independent overview of these decisions is necessary.

initiatives, often held back because of the lack of start-up finance.

The EU's research into renewable energies could be enhanced by cutting down on nuclear fission R&D. This is a massive and mature industry which needs weaning from its over-dependence on state hand-outs. Renewables need to rise up the priority list since the potential gains are vastly in excess of those from nuclear fission.

R&D has considerable impact upon the society in which we live and one of the welcome innovations within the Fourth Framework programme is the creation of 'targeted socio-economic research', to facilitate the integration of R&D into society and to forecast and anticipate future change. Until now, this aspect has been largely a matter of reacting to changes that have sometimes had very drastic effects upon society. As we move further into the 'information age', it is necessary to be more pro-active. What changes will take place because of biotechnological developments in farming and in pharmacy? What will happen to the EU coal industries with or without clean-coal technology? Clean-coal technologies can open up markets in China and Eastern Europe and so produce jobs in the EU. How will vulnerable and disadvantaged groups be affected by the advance of technology? These socio-economic questions will at last have some funding and structure to enable the management of technological change.

The EU is in touch with networks of researchers all over the world. These contacts are particularly extensive in underdeveloped countries with a view to helping them find solutions to their own problems in agriculture and natural resources management. This is not purely altruism, but gives the EU a detailed knowledge of potential markets. Central and Eastern Europe and the newly independent states are also beneficiaries of this same programme combined with other EU initiatives such as PHARE. This is another budget priority.

The bureaucracy of the bid process is a cause of great complaint. But the system needs to keep track of the many thousands of projects and clearly state what each project and partner within the project is supposed to do. To this end, the bureaucracy is being refined. Monitoring and evaluation, an essential part of each project, is currently being improved. Technological trajectories require adjustment between the start of a programme and its completion.

JRC

The EU has its own laboratory – the Joint Research Centre. It presently consists of eight separate laboratories on five different sites. It has specialist expertise in the fields of nuclear fission safety, the environment and climate and 60% of the 600 million ecu yearly cost is for these subjects. The effectiveness of this internal research has received very poor reports. The situation is being improved, but the future lies more with external R&D.

Dissemination

Research is not enough. The results must also be disseminated – very difficult in practice. The technology-based Small and Medium Enterprises (SMEs) often have neither the time nor the knowledge to find and study research results that could well be of great benefit. Yet the hope of the Delors White Paper was that these SMEs would provide many new jobs. There are over thirteen million SMEs and it would take many times the present resources to disseminate results effectively, even amongst those involved with technology. Dissemination and distribution of results to all companies, small and large, has to be given greater emphasis.

Added Value

Of what benefit is this R&D expenditure to EU community citizens? What is the 'added value' of R&D which comes from co-operative effort on a European scale? One could simply point out that if £1 million of R&D can be shared amongst, say, five partners, each one has to invest only 20% of the cost and yet gains the results of knowledge and expertise of the £1 million. Even better for each partner is that the EU pays 50% of the cost so that each individual partner pays only £100,000 – just 10% of the project cost. An EU R&D project is always multinational and thereby builds up relationships and networks which increase the social and technological cohesiveness of Europe. Further, there is a gentle bias towards accepting partners from regions marginally lagging behind in R&D which enables them to take a higher profile than would be possible if they were left to their own resources.

Giving a Stronger Voice to R&D

The Fifth Framework programme, due to start in 1999, needs to be reassessed. Currently there are three strands of public R&D funding: (a) national government programmes; (b) free-standing European Centres such as CERN and ESA; and (c) the European Union Framework programme. Alongside these are by far the largest stakeholders in R&D – individual businesses and industries. There is growing co-operation between these strands and private industry, but further improvements are needed. The EU should be allowed to co-ordinate nearly all European public R&D. The EUREKA programme must be integrated within the Fifth Framework Programme; and COST, a parallel co-ordinating body, needs to be integrated with the EU. The practice of putting in bids to both EUREKA and Framework Programmes only perpetuates bureaucracy with no benefits to R&D.

An objective of shared research is to lower the cost of R&D and to reduce duplication. The EU has been given the task – agreed by all participating countries – of co-ordinating the Community's and member states' R&D activities and, in close co-operation with member states, take any useful initiative to this end (article 130h). The Commission can act here as 'honest broker'.

We want a single 'European Voice for Research and Technology'. The EU must lead a concerted effort to form centres of excellence in each key sector, such as the automobiles' renewable energy sector, next generation aircraft, high-speed trains. It would be prudent to use existing facilities and reinforce them as necessary. They must be 'distributed centres of excellence' with facilities spread over several sites in different member states. Their remit would be to link directly with universities and industries throughout the EU and be the leading authoritative body for R&D within the particular sector. Each would be the 'European Voice' for its sector. Realistically it is only the EU that can establish such a comprehensive set of sectoral centres of excellence. Individual member states do not have all the sectors and individual manufacturers lack the resources. The EU has the expertise and the authority to carry out such a task.

These centres of excellence could be the basis for helping the European Parliament and the Commission to form and modulate policy in such matters as the direction of research, legislation over intellectual property rights and patenting, and to act as the 'Voice of the EU for Research and Technological Development' upon the world stage. If the EU is to take the lead in production and marketing of high-technology goods, then such an institution is vital.

Parliament must also develop its own sources of advice in scientific and technological matters. STOA, the Science and Technology Office of Assessment, offers an embryo body. The need for such a parliamentary counterweight is highlighted by the 'task force' concept of Edith Cresson, the Research Commissioner, in co-operation with the Industry Commissioner, Martin Bangemann, and Neil Kinnock, Commissioner for Transport. They are trying to co-ordinate various bodies and organizations within five particular topics: 'the car of tomorrow', 'educational software multimedia', 'new generation aircraft', 'vaccines and viral diseases' and 'the train of the future'. The concept has many good points, but it has been introduced almost as a whim, without democratic control and with consequent unauthorized re-ordering of expenditure already earmarked within the Fourth Framework. It is vital that industrial competitiveness policies are 'owned' by all the EU institutions (Commission, Parliament and Council) as well as the research and industrial communities. The directions that EU R&D take must not be subjugated to sudden unilateral initiatives by Commissioners even though, as in this particular case, such proposals may have merit. Additionally, these task forces will restrict R&D in other areas such as renewable energy sources. The European Parliament must be the 'watch-dog' that protects our citizens from such *ad hoc* use of public funds.

Our R&D must serve us better. We have to ensure that *all* our citizens' lives are enhanced by R&D and not just those in selected areas of the community. We have to build a more rational structure to R&D than the one we have inherited from our individual member states. We have to cherish the growing links between research workers in different parts of the community, because they are helping to build the cohesiveness that is the cement of the Europe of the next millennium. Most importantly, we want to address the democratic deficit in R&D and we want to put it near the top of our financial priorities.

ARLENE McCARTHY
A Europe of the Regions: Building Economic and Social Cohesion in Britain and Europe

As Britain moves towards the next millennium, eighteen years of Conservative centralism and economic mismanagement have seen many of our once prosperous regions spiral into economic and social decline.

For a party and government which preaches the values of 'one nation' and maintaining the Union, the Conservatives have presided over a period of widening North–South divide. They have been solely responsible for tearing the Union asunder and weakening the commitment to national solidarity as people and local areas fight for their own economic survival. Even the South and the traditionally Tory heartlands of Middle England have seen a decline in their economic fortunes, with deepening recession and job losses. Within the more prosperous parts of Britain, there are now pockets of severe deprivation. The divide within regions is growing and creating an underlying current of economic and social tension which has already manifested itself in rising crime, public unrest and a deep sense of economic insecurity. Yet in the key indicator of unemployment, regional differences are narrowing as a result of negative convergence: the gap is closing because, in traditionally low-unemployment regions, unemployment is rising. Berkshire, for example, had an unemployment rate in 1990 of 2.5%. In 1995 this reached 6%. Merseyside's rate of unemployment remains high at 14.3%, not far behind that of Northern Ireland with a figure of 14.8%. The EU average for the same period of 1992–1994 is 10.2%.

The result of a *laissez-faire* economic policy and inadequate regional policy has led UK regions to depend on European regional grant aid. In many regions, this is the biggest single force for investment. It has reached the stage now whereby every region in the UK has some assisted areas.[1]

In 1993, for the first time, the UK increased its geographical coverage for European regional aid. Two new areas were added to the list of Objective 1 regions in Europe, i.e. those areas deemed to be lagging behind: Merseyside and Highlands and Islands. Many more rural areas were designated (under Objective 5b status) as in need of European regional support and, of course, the list of industrial areas qualifying for support remained substantial (see Appendices 1 and 2 to this chapter).

The European Union's Rechar Programme, aimed at the restructuring of coalfield areas, saw the UK qualify for the highest allocation of aid in Europe, in the wake of the government's coal closure programme which resulted in extensive job losses. What the government often portrays as a success story in lobbying for and attracting European funds, in reality masks a deep economic and social malaise in Britain's regions, placing us high up the league table of Europe's poorest regions – a damning indictment of Conservative economic policy and their disregard for the needs of the regions.

---

[1] House of Commons, Trade and Industry Committee Fourth Report, Regional Policy HC356-I. HMSO, 29 March, 1995.

Making the Transition from Failure to Success

The challenge for a new Labour Government will be to translate Europe's policy of economic and social cohesion into a nationally sponsored cohesion policy for Britain's regions.

While the UK under the Conservatives has rejected an interventionist or redistributive policy to support declining regions, Europe has moved closer to a stronger and more active regional policy. In 1975, only 4.8% of the EC's budget was dedicated to regional policy. In 1993, expenditure accounted for 31%. By 1999, almost 36% of the Union's total budget will be invested in regional aid. Spending on agriculture will decline over the same period from 51% to 46% of the total. Regional policy is competing fiercely with the discredited CAP as a more productive and effective way to support Europe's regions, both urban and rural, and to enhance their competitiveness in the global market-place.

As a European policy, economic and social cohesion is not new. Its origins go back to the founding days of the European Union, when the Treaty of Rome included in its preamble the objective of 'harmonious development by reducing the differences between various regions and by mitigating the backwardness of less favoured regions.' In the 1950s, with a Community of just six members and economic prosperity, it was not deemed necessary to set a strong interventionist regional policy as an adjunct to national economic policy. Support was only forthcoming for a policy which would top-up funding to weaker regions, and which would not interfere unduly in member states' prerogatives to tackle regional economic problems on a purely national basis. In essence, the goal was to achieve better co-ordination of regional policies throughout Europe, between member states, and indeed, better co-ordination of those policies conducted at European level with a regional impact. There was then no distinct European model of regional policy. However, with subsequent enlargement in the 1980s, including some southern and the Mediterranean countries, Europe incorporated areas with weak regions, and the disparities between poor and prosperous regions grew.

It is ironic that in 1973, under the Conservatives, Britain, as one of the most centralized member states in the Community, was responsible through its Commissioner for Regional Affairs for producing a document which recommended the need for a European Regional Policy.[2] The negotiations themselves were to take place with Labour in government, albeit with a small majority. At that time, the nine member states had to thrash out the proposals and identify how much money should be involved in a European Regional Development Fund; which areas should be eligible for support; how allocations would be fixed; and which criteria should be used. The final thrust was given by the Irish and Italian governments, who threatened to boycott the Paris Summit if there was not an immediate pledge to create a European Regional Development Fund (ERDF). The Summit endorsed this and the ERDF was established in 1975.

Economic recession in the 1970s and early 1980s made divisions between winners and losers even more pronounced, and so it was as much through economic necessity as the drive towards a single European market that moves were made to reinforce economic and social cohesion and to include regional policy as a common European policy in subsequent treaty changes.

[2] Commission 'On the Problems of the Enlarged Community' COM 127, 5 May, 1973.

The economic arguments for regional policy have strengthened over the years. The commitment to EMU in the early 1970s was made with the widespread recognition that major regional imbalances could prevent implementation of a Single Market and Economic and Monetary Union. The only solution, to bring these regions up to the level of the rest of Europe, was to propose a more comprehensive policy of regional aid. The 1987 Single European Act resulted in a commitment to economic and social cohesion because it held that economic integration would create a 'golden triangle' at the geographical core of Europe, a high-growth and high-investment area. Most of Europe's economic activity would be sucked into this zone and exacerbate the problem of declining and peripheral regions.

In the 1990s, the Single Market, Economic and Monetary Union and a strong regional policy share the objective of improving Europe's economic competitiveness and performance. The legal basis for economic and social cohesion is firmly anchored in Article 130 of the Maastricht Treaty. This states that to establish a Single European Market, there is a need for common policies and activities to promote a harmonious and balanced development: 'To promote the raising of the standard of living and quality of life, the Community shall aim at reducing disparities between levels of development of the various regions and the backwardness of least favoured regions including rural areas.'

A Policy of Solidarity

Economic and social cohesion is the cornerstone of the left's policy of solidarity in Europe; of ensuring that Europe does not only benefit the few, but that the benefits of being part of a European Union spreads out across all regions. The fundamental basis of the left's philosophy is to reject gross inequality, and to reject it not only for moral reasons but also because it has a negative impact on the overall health of the economy through the unacceptable cost of poverty, unemployment and lack of competitiveness.

Economic and social cohesion is vital for securing the support of all members of the EU for European integration. A loose association of states involved in a free trade area and exchange of goods would not result in a widespread share of the benefits for all, but rather in an exclusive club for the more prosperous areas, increasing their share of prosperity on the back of the poorer regions. Such a scenario would not only be unacceptable to the left; logically it would not find favour with poorer member states, even with those governed by right-wing governments. It would be equally difficult to imagine Chancellor Kohl arguing for less solidarity or cohesion if it meant that the new German Länder were to lose out on vital European support for regional economic development. Moreover, good economic sense dictates that an upturn in the economic fortunes of Europe's poorer regions would have a positive impact for the richer regions; it would allow the poorer regions to trade with, and import goods from, the wealthier regions, thus creating a virtuous cycle of economic regeneration across the board. Regional policy which relies on net contributions to the Union's budget, and which thereby allows for transfers to the weaker states, has an overall positive impact on the European economy, and should be seen as a policy of enlightened self-interest.

The Union has a range of financial mechanisms and support programmes which underpin the objective of economic and social cohesion and which constitute an overall co-ordinated regional strategy. Of these, the most substantial are the Structural Funds. The funds devoted to structural policies, as a result of the deal struck at the Edinburgh Summit, will increase by 41%, from 21 billion ecu in 1993 to 30 billion ecu in 1999. Total commitments have more than doubled from 63,727 million ecu in the period 1989–1993 to 141,471 million ecu for 1994–1999.[3]

The Union has travelled a long way from the modest 4.8% of the budget reserved for Structural Fund actions in 1975. Not only has the overall budget allocation changed, but the operation of the funds has been subject to several reforms. Initially, funds were allocated on the basis of national quotas, and member states enjoyed the exclusive right of designating their own areas for financial support. Often grants were only of the order of 10–30% of the total project cost. And, as has been noted elsewhere, 'In the UK the greater benefit from the fund accrued to the Treasury rather than the public authority in question'.[4]

Reform at the end of the 1970s and in the 1980s saw a shift away from regional policy which funded national regional programmes by a system of quotas. In part, this was in recognition of the fact that insufficient progress was being made in overcoming regional disparities, that resources were being spread too thinly across too many areas. National quotas were replaced by two types of

---

[3] Commission 'From the Single Act to Maastricht and Beyond – The Means to Match our Ambitions' COM(92) 2000.

[4] Spicers European Union Policy Briefings 'Regional Policy' – Jill Preston p.28.

programmes – the National Programme of Community Interest (NPCI) and the Community Programme (CP) – marking a shift away from individual priority projects by national member states to a broader-based strategic programming approach to regional development. These programmes were drawn up by the member states in consultation with local authorities and regions and were concentrated in member states' own assisted areas. Ultimately, they led to a process of strategic, multi-annual programming over a period of three to five years.

By the time the 1988 reforms came into being, following the SEA, it was clear that Europe wanted strong, strategic, integrated regional programmes as the main plank of European Regional Policy. These would be co-ordinated with national policies but would also represent a distinct European response to growing regional disparities.

Recent Reforms of the Structural Funds

The overall impact of successive reforms has led to the creation of a European Regional Policy which is more strategically focused, concentrating its resources on the poorer peripheral areas, and which seeks to involve local authorities and regions in its decision-making processes.

The 1988 reforms established the current priorities for Structural Funds:

- Objective 1: concentrated on those areas lagging behind; regions whose per capita GDP is less than 75% of the Community average over three years
- Objective 2: concentrated on those areas seriously affected by industrial decline, where the average rate of unemployment is above the Community average, where there is a higher percentage of industrial employment

than the EU average, and where there is a decline in industrial employment
- Objective 3: directed towards the long-term unemployed, i.e. workers over twenty-five years who have been unemployed for more than twelve months
- Objective 4: concerned with the integration of young people and with youth unemployment
- Objective 5a: adapting production, processing and marketing structures in agriculture and forestry
- Objective 5b: promoting the development of rural areas

With the addition of three new member states to the European Union in 1994, a further objective was created:

- Objective 6: for Arctic regions which are particularly sparsely populated.

The Commission was given the right of initiative in selecting eligible areas.

For the first time, the concept of partnership was incorporated into the regulations governing the implementation of the Structural Funds, with a view to getting local and regional authorities more closely and actively involved. Monitoring committees were established to oversee the implementation of the programmes. These monitoring committees were to be drawn from a broad range of representatives from the member states' regional or local governments and the Commission. The role of these committees was (and is) to select and endorse projects, and to monitor the implementation of measures contained within the CSF. In the UK, the secretariat of the committees are civil servants from the Integrated Regional Offices.

A controversial dimension to rules governing the use of Structural Funds is that of 'additionality'. Effectively, this means that member states are no longer able to fund the Treasury via European regional grants; for every £1 of

European grant which comes into a region, they are expected to match this with £1 of additional public funds. The Conservatives are reluctant to comply with the principle of additionality, seeing European grants as a convenient substitution for national funds. As a result, additionality continues to cause problems between the UK and the Commission.

Another new departure in 1988 was the decision to set up Community Initiatives, with 10% of the overall regional fund budget set aside to address the specific problems of industrial crisis areas: coal; steel; shipbuilding; the environment; textiles; the defence industry; and two new programmes, NOW (equal opportunities for women in the labour market) and Horizon (access to the labour market for people with disabilities and minority groups). A further aim was to encourage inter-regional networking, transnational co-operation and cross-border co-operation. The Delors II package sought to reinforce the link between cohesion and competitiveness. Even though the gap between the more prosperous and the poorer regions was being bridged in terms of economic growth statistics, regional policy had not been effective in tackling unemployment disparities in the regions. Growth rates have increased in the poorest regions of Ireland, Portugal and Spain, for example, but this has not been translated into job creation. In 1986 the twenty-five poorest regions had an average unemployment rate five times higher than the twenty-five wealthiest regions. This trend worsened, so that by 1993 the ten worst affected regions had an unemployment rate seven times higher (25.3%) than the wealthiest regions (3.6%).

The main thrust of the 1993 reform package sought to achieve greater concentrations of resources into the regions in need; programming as an integrated strategic approach;

the strengthening of partnerships to include participatory democracy; the greater involvement of local authorities and social partners in the decision-making process linked to the allocation of grants; and additionality to ensure that grants from Europe are truly additional and do not replace national grants to the regions, thus saving the Treasury additional expenditure. This reform also took place against the backdrop of growing concern about intolerable and rising levels of unemployment in the regions.

Some large-scale European-funded projects have caused serious environmental damage, particularly in Greece, Spain, Portugal and Ireland, as have the UK's road building schemes (funded by ERDF). Parliament asked for stronger environmental impact assessments to be included in Structural Fund programmes. An equal opportunities clause was also incorporated into the regulations which govern the Structural Funds, to ensure better scope for women and socially-excluded groups to benefit from the funds. Finally, the reform of the funds led to the establishment of the Cohesion Fund (Article 130d of the Maastricht Treaty) for the four poorer states of Ireland, Greece, Portugal and Spain, to aid economic convergence of these states in the run-up to EMU. It is the member states and not the regions which look after these funds and which select projects for support at a higher grant level of at least 80% of the overall cost of the project. This fund targets transport and environmental projects.

Some changes were undertaken to the focus and actions of the specific funds. The old Objectives 3 and 4, designed for training and employment initiatives, were combined to combat the problem of the long-term unemployed and the integration of young people and the socially marginalized. A new Objective 4 was created which, instead of tackling unemployment after the event, attempted to anticipate future structural problems in industries by retraining workers already in employment to adapt to industrial change and new production systems.

The UK government objected to this programme and refused to implement it. To date, over £60 million of grants go unclaimed. The logic is difficult to comprehend. While a satisfactory response has not been forthcoming as to why the government has not taken up this initiative, several assumptions could be made, to fit in with Conservative economic dogma. To select certain companies for European public subsidies would go against the grain of the free market and would be seen as anti-competitive. Moreover, the Treasury and government departments would not benefit from this fund as grants would be available to the industry concerned. However, such an initiative from Europe would be an ideal incentive to encourage local and regional industry to engage in the fight against unemployment by encouraging them to do more in-house training. These European-stimulated initiatives could nurture a sense of local responsibility by industries for the development of the local and regional economy. Competitiveness in the regions relies as much on the training and adaptation of the current work-force as on the creation of new opportunities.

The issue of subsidiarity, which has been hotly debated across the Union, has played a significant role in the debate on regional policy. In essence, and specifically in the case of the UK, it is a fundamental question of who is in control. Since 1975, the Commission has gained more influence in directing and determining the priorities of regional policy and has taken the lead in launching new regional initiatives. However the member states retain the final say.

In the 1993 reform of the Structural Funds, subsidiarity meant that member states had a stronger role. In drawing up the list for Objective 2 eligible areas, the member states themselves propose the areas. A process of negotiation with the Commission follows, but the Commission is not in a position to add new areas to the list, or to propose additional areas. Objective 1-eligible areas, by contrast, are determined by the Council of Ministers. The implementation of the European grant programmes remains the preserve of the member state. It is the responsibility of integrated regional offices, under instruction from London, to determine policy in the regions. Subsidiarity is confined to pulling back decisions to Whitehall from Brussels; it does not stretch to granting a role for local authorities or local economic actors in the development of regional strategies, plans or programmes. But in any event, the notion of Europe interfering in the 'nooks and crannies' of national, let alone regional, decisions is clearly unfounded.

We know Europe has become increasingly important to our regions as a source of funding for local economic development as central government grants to our regions diminish. Regional policy is a visible, tangible policy which enjoys popular support in Europe's regions. But a region's interest in Europe is not only about accessing funds, it is also about developing a strategic and coherent approach at regional level to legislation emanating from Brussels, in such diverse areas as environment, education, agriculture, public health, transport and public procurement. It is about shaping the development of a Europe of the regions. Without a strategic approach at regional level, there is little scope to influence policy processes before they arrive at the final stages of legislation, and so ensure that policies and programmes support and develop cohesion within and between regions.

The Challenge for Britain's Regions

Regions also need to strengthen their participation and involvement in the Single European Market and actively network in inter-regional partnerships. Many UK regions have taken up the challenge and opened up regional offices close to the Commission and Parliament buildings in Brussels, with a view to improving the flow of information back to the regions. As a result, they are in a better position to respond to the challenge of legislation. More importantly, they are well-placed to take advantage of the new opportunities in Europe. The European Commission has acknowledged the role of regional offices by providing regular briefings across a range of policy areas.

Whitehall civil servants and government ministers have reacted nervously to the establishment of regional offices, fearing an attempt to bypass central government machinery. The reality is that the regions have adapted to the creation and further consolidation of a Europe of the Regions. The setting-up of the Committee of the Regions, under Article 198 of the Maastricht Treaty, was a further step in this process. The UK now needs a regional response and regional structures in order to get the best out of these new structures in Europe. The government's eleven new integrated regional offices have not shown an interest in developing a voice for the UK regions in Europe; instead, they have got on with the mundane machinery of implementing European programmes while adhering to instructions from Whitehall. They perceive their job as representing Whitehall in the regions rather than to represent the regions' interests either in Whitehall or Brussels.

For the left, the task of achieving economic and social cohesion through a pro-active regional policy has to go hand-in-hand with increased democracy in our regions, an enhanced role for regional and local actors to participate in their own regeneration, and more transparency in the implementation of funding programmes. Transparency is necessary to allow us to judge whether funds are being used in an accountable manner, and also whether efficient use is being made of European funds.

Socialists in the European Parliament's Regional Affairs Committee have taken the task of monitoring the use of funds in our regions as a serious and key component of the Committee's scrutiny role. While the Commission is the guardian of the treaties, the European Parliament is a staunch defender of citizens' and regions' interests. The Parliament has a clear mandate to insist on more democratic and transparent practices, for, while the Commission and the Court of Auditors carry out reports and monitoring, neither of them are democratically elected bodies, nor do they owe an allegiance to Europe's citizens or local authorities and regions.

The clear dividing line between the European right and the European left in the Parliament is not a division over the need for a regional policy but over the principles of application. Partnership is not a priority for the right. The right does not want partnership which involves social partners and in particular the trade union representatives' involvement in decisions on European grants. In our approach to the 1996 Intergovernmental Conference, in addition to a strengthened role for economic and social cohesion and a stronger role for Europe's regions in the decision-making processes, we want to see the principles of democracy, partnership and accountability firmly applied to the conduct of regional policy.

Nowhere is the implementation of regional policy more undemocratic and unaccountable than in the UK. The

Programme Monitoring Committees (PMCs) which endorse eligible projects for European funding are renowned for their undemocratic working practices, which makes it difficult to evaluate them.

The Conservative Approach: The Dead Hand of Central Government

In the past, the Conservative Government has been in breach of the additionality principle, by which every £1 of European grant must be matched by £1 from government. Instead, the government has used the funds to replace spending which should have been allocated to the regions in any case, thereby subsidizing the lack of national regional policy. The former Labour Commissioner, Bruce Millan, took a hard line with the government and blocked funds to the coal regions from the EU's Rechar Programme until the government provided guarantees that local authorities eligible for grants would receive extra spending power. The then Secretary of State for Trade and Industry, Peter Lilley, announced a major shift in policy in February 1992, shortly before the General Election. All the evidence suggested – and leaked letters from Michael Heseltine indicated – that withholding funds to the regions would not be a vote-winner for the Conservatives and a speedy resolution was necessary.

It is not clear whether the Conservatives have solved their problem with additionality in European funds. The matching contribution has to be found within a local authority's own spending thresholds. This means that local authorities have to cut back on other projects in order to be able to take up European grants. Savage cuts in credit approvals and strict controls in the use of capital receipts mean local authorities have difficulty in finding any cash to match European grants. This is compounded by the strait-jacket of unfair and tough local government settlements in the annual budgets, which has forced local authorities to make cuts in the provision of frontline services even before contemplating the finance required to run European projects. The risk is that, unable to find matching funds in local authority coffers, grants will go unclaimed, resulting in a massive underspend. European grants would then be lost to the regions.

To avoid this, the government allowed national grants – for example, City Challenge and the Single Regeneration Budget – to be used for matching funds. More significantly, the government opened up grant access to a whole range of governmental agencies and even allowed the privatized utilities to apply for funds. This meant the priority of funding would be led by national schemes in the regions, and funding would go to utilities whose profit margins post-privatization meant that matching funding for projects was readily available. In short, grants are not geared towards the priorities of the local economic actors in the regions; they are skewed towards national schemes, towards making up the shortfall in publicly financed agencies, and towards paying for improved maintenance work by the privatized utilities. Given the profit margins of the latter, this hardly represents allocation of funds on the basis of need.

The core problem – as in so many areas – is that European regional policy in the UK is Treasury-driven. European grants should not be designed to help the Treasury bankroll the PSBR; rather, they should form a financial element of a coherent strategy driven by industrial, employment and regional policy considerations. Everywhere, the dead hand of central government stifles participation and innovation. Additionality rules continue to be breached. In October 1995, the Welsh Office was taken to task by the Commissioner for Regional Affairs for replacing grants to the Welsh Development Agency (WDA) with European grants. The Commission responded by blocking grants to Wales until the Welsh Office provide clear audit lines which prove they are not substituting national cash with European cash.

John Major's pledge for open government has been revealed as a hollow public relations exercise. The UK government does not meet the principles of democracy, partnership, accountability; the jury is still out on additionality, with blatant cases of rule breaches coming to light. Currently, at the request of MEPs,[5] the Commission is investigating the allocation of European grants to the privatized utilities. Between 1985 and 1994, the amount of grant absorbed by the utilities was almost £1/2 billion. Gas, water, telecommunications and electricity have received substantial payments from the European Regional Development Fund. The Commission needs to determine the extent to which the payment of public subsidies enhanced the sale of the utilities by providing a sweetener. Furthermore, government must explain why the privatized utilities have been allowed to directly draw on millions of pounds of grant post-privatization, when they are clearly a private-sector company. Recent discussions with government offices revealed that one reason for not allowing the private sector a stronger role was the fear that private companies would have access to windfall profits. Here the government is flexibly applying its own rules regarding the private sector's access to European grants. Small private-sector companies in the regions are not allowed direct grant sup-

---

[5] Oral Question by Arlene McCarthy H-0328/95 on Privatization of Public Utilities and the European Regional Development Fund, 26 April, 1995.

port from the ERDF; in fact, they are positively discouraged from getting involved in programmes in their regions. By contrast, private utilities appear to have preferential access, with a right to a place on the monitoring committee.

The fact that privatized utilities have benefited from large amounts of European cash underlines the weakness of the democratic structures in allocating funds and the lack of transparency. Every million spent propping up the government's privatization programme – British Rail benefited from £19 million in Euro grants over the same period – is robbing the regions of valuable resources for small-scale projects which could have had a greater impact locally and may have provided better value for money – the government's own criteria. People in our regions have to see a benefit from European funds. The skills and potential energy of local people and local economic actors remain largely untapped.

Small and medium-sized enterprises should be allowed a more active role in the process. European Social Funds, designed to fund and target local training needs, provide further examples of the government sequestering these grants for their own initiatives. ESF grants to the regions are held back for national training schemes, i.e. Youth Training and Training to Work. In some areas, over 40% of these grants are committed to schemes originating in London and not in the regions. This makes it difficult for local innovative schemes to compete on a level playing-field. If the government offices in the regions are drawing up selection criteria to favour their own schemes, 'The requirement on government offices to make successful bids should be taken into account when determining selection criteria.'[6]

---

[6] Local Government Chronicle 'Scheming for a Slice of Europe's Cash', David Haggie, 6 October, 1995, pp 16–17.

Even government agencies such as the Training and Enterprise Councils have been given to understand that if they produce local projects which compete with the government's national schemes in the region, they may have their statutory funding removed. 'The addition of TECs as another competitor for regional ESF money will inevitably put pressure on government bids ... If the level of TEC bids were to threaten the success of government applications, the potential effect on the employment department's budget and the probable effect on the TECs' budgets should be explained to the TECs and they should be encouraged not to submit or to withdraw their bids'[7]

Decision-making bodies should include social partners, employers and trade unions, and elected members from the local authorities. Members should be drawn from a democratic process of self-selection and not appointed by government heads of the integrated regional offices.

The Labour Response: Unlocking the Potential of the Regions

Labour will have to break through the undemocratic quangos which currently control and dispense our European grants in the regions, and return a sense of ownership of these European programmes to people. The principle of partnership cannot be exclusive. Audit trails should be established to ensure transparency in the allocation and spending of European funding. A ruling on the status of privatized utilities should be made. If they are engaging in projects which are of benefit to the public, they should still compete on equal terms with other public projects. A

[7] Ibid

Labour Government should ensure that decisions are taken in the regions. They must abandon the current practice of top-slicing funds for nationally sponsored schemes which do not match the needs of the regions. They must abandon the Conservatives' glossy gameshow approach to allocating regional funds such as City Challenge and Regional Challenge. The allocation of regional funds should not be conducted as a lottery. The development of our regions is for future generations, and the need to secure their competitive future in a Europe of the Regions is much too serious for a frivolous winner-takes-all approach.

The problem we encounter with the Regional Challenge scheme as an approach to allocating European funds is that it creates additional bureaucracy both locally and at a national level which is wholly superfluous. It is yet another way to top-slice European grants and return decision-making to Whitehall, creating yet more tiers of centralized bureaucracy. As a philosophy of regional public policy, it divides winners from losers and fails to encourage a sense of dynamism in our regions. The players are often disillusioned, because it is difficult to see that funds have been allocated according to any objective criteria of need or opportunity. That in itself creates a sense of division and tension in our regions. A competitive tension promotes regeneration, but not if central government interference means decisions are weighted.

The role of government in our regions is to enable and bring to fruition schemes which are locally engendered and to provide the macroeconomic conditions which promote regional and local economic development. Developments in Europe mean that we cannot take for granted the policy gains made in achieving a stronger European Regional Policy to offset the negative impacts of the Single European Market. But economic and social cohesion and the concept of solidarity is under threat from the right, as seen in the creeping process of deregulation and liberalization. Solidarity with Europe's poorer regions is more difficult to achieve when the wealthier member states are reluctant to maintain the current level of budgetary contributions. The larger member states would like to renationalize European regional funds completely, and go back to the old system of national quotas, which would give governments a free rein in allocating funds in the regions.

The UK's debate in the House of Commons on contributions to the European Union Budget opened up the old Tory divisions on Europe. Teresa Gorman led the charge with her pamphlet 'Not One Penny More'. The whip was removed from nine Tory MPs for refusing to vote for budgetary contributions to the EU budget, despite representing only 1.1% of GNP. Ironically, it was John Major who helped put together the package which involved a financial commitment at Edinburgh in 1992 to double contributions to Structural Funds by 1999. Budgetary contributions will continue to be a contentious issue across all EU member states. The Dutch government has not yet ratified the increase in the budget and is holding out for a better financial deal with the promise of a potential rebate via other Community sources of funding.

Future Labour ministers will need to decide if it should be a priority to maintain the EU budget contribution at its current level, let alone allowing for increases. If we are to make an impact on unemployment levels in the Union, then we have to use our current levels of funding in a more effective way. Prudent financial management is called for. Limited and valuable European grants should not be used to prop up ailing administrations, nor should they fund large infrastructure schemes which are the proper responsibility of national governments. The grants should not be used to give preferential treatment to certain sectors over others, nor to fund Treasury deficits.

Current funds which are available to our regions via Europe should be better integrated and co-ordinated to ensure maximum impact. The administrative processes by which projects are allocated funds in Brussels and Whitehall should be stringent enough to prevent fraud and wastage, but not so restrictive as to prevent local areas from having access to funds and getting programmes up and running, as has been the current government's practice. Almost two years elapsed between the agreement of new programmes for the UK, and the decision in English Objective 2 regions to give approval to the first projects. Interminable delays are undermining the impact of European grants in the regions.

As the European Union moves inexorably towards a Europe of the Regions, the lack of an appropriate regional structure in the UK for the development and articulation of views and the administration of public policy becomes all the more problematic. The proliferation of government competition only serves to distract from the real issues of tackling problems at their root.

With the downgrading of regional policy in the last decade and the confused, ambiguous approach which leads to waste and duplication as more and more quangos decide the future direction of economic and social policy in our regions, Labour's proposals for the regions are critical to future dynamism and democracy.

The Future of Europe's Regions – The Challenge of Enlargement and EMU

Europe's regional policy is changing at a rapid pace. The addition of three new member states in January 1995 means the territorial area within which regional policy operates has been expanded to include 370 million citizens. Countries in Central and Eastern Europe, to say nothing of Malta and Cyprus, are waiting for membership. Enlargement to the east will have a far-reaching impact on the cohesion policy of the Union. For the UK, the centre of gravity of the Union will move further east, putting us in a more peripheral position, geographically speaking. In terms of these new countries' structural problems, it would require a substantial share of regional funds to close the gap – more than the EU has at its disposal. Structural Fund expenditure would rise from 25 billion ecu to 60 billion ecu. Who will fund this when budgetary rigour is the order of the day? The principle of concentration means that Britain would no longer qualify for structural grants. The Union and the left must develop a strategic and responsible approach to enlargement. It is our goal to create an open Europe – accessible to all citizens – but we have to seek to preserve the integrity of the Union. The right wants rapid enlargement because it will weaken economic and social cohesion, and do away with solidarity.

The left needs to guard against falling into a trap which will take us back to the days before Maastricht, with a free trade zone, exclusive market approach and intergovernmentalism. Labour has to argue for enlargement in a manageable time-span. The most important service we can give Central and Eastern Europe is to ensure access to EU markets to permit regeneration in their own economies. We need to underpin and further support the processes of democratic and economic renewal by promoting such initiatives as the PHARE, ECOS and Ouverture Programmes. While the politicians debate and deliberate, local authorities and regions are already making a strong contribution to future enlargement by linking up with Central and Eastern Europe, through exchange of experience and co-operation programmes across a broad range of policy areas, including the environment, small business development, and tourism.

These co-operative and integrational structures should be expanded in preparation for a smooth transition to further enlargement of the Union. To argue for rapid enlargement would risk the gains already made in maintaining high standards in environmental and social legislation. It cannot be in the interests of the left to weaken these hard-fought advances in European policy. Regional policy itself would come under considerable strain to meet the new financial demands and some member states would find ammunition for their argument to abandon regional policy as unworkable and financially not viable.

Economic and Monetary Union will provide stability for Europe's regions and help businesses by reducing transaction costs. However, unless we consolidate our regional policy, there is a risk that EMU could lead to a widening of regional economic disparities. The convergence criteria require a high degree of fiscal discipline. This will have an impact on regions through its effects on national economic policy. The pressure on public deficits could mean less national expenditure in regions. Rejecting EMU is not the answer. A multi-speed Europe would allow core countries to proceed with integration, allowing them to cut loose from their obligation to help poorer regions meet the criteria and thereby undermining economic and social cohesion.

The challenge is to adapt our regional policies to promote cohesion alongside EMU, and to enhance regional economic competitiveness by greater involvement of local economic actors in Structural Fund programmes. At institutional level, an incoming Labour Government should be arguing for the treaty provisions for economic and social cohesion to be strengthened. It would be desirable to set up a Cohesion Institute as a counterweight to the EMI and the Central Bank. Cohesion policies could be supported through borrowing on international capital markets and providing low-interest loans or development funds to poorer regions, without having to increase EU budgetary contributions. There are strong arguments for such an institution and for the creation of a European Investment Fund – allowing regions to draw on such a fund for regional regeneration programmes.[8]

Labour in Europe: The Future of Britain's Regions

As Europe continues to evolve from a free trade area to an internal market, to an economic, social and political union, via treaty reforms and the Intergovernmental Conference in 1996, there is a recognition that people do not always understand what these changes signify in terms of their own lives. This was clear from the debates over the Maastricht Treaty reform, where citizens did not comprehend which policies were being pushed in their name, nor why these policies were relevant to them. The distance between citizens and the place where decisions are taken often results in a gap of understanding between European

---

[8] *The European Imperative, Economic and Social Cohesion in the 1990s*, Stuart Holland, Russell Press Ltd, Nottingham, October 1993.

institutions and our citizens. This can lead to Euro-scepticism and open hostility to all things European. We cannot hope to bridge that gap without a strong role for local government in Europe, and without a strong strategic role for local authorities in our UK regions. We need to take Europe to the people.

The growing trend in the UK to marginalize democratically-elected local authorities – to hand over decisions and give increasing access to funds to unelected quangos – is one which will not serve the needs and interests of our citizens in local areas. Coupled with an increasing centralization of power in Whitehall, the trend is to downgrade the role of local authorities. Further constraints of finance for local government hamper its work. It is indeed remarkable that, against all the odds, UK local government has been playing an active role in Europe; it is able to hold its own alongside our European counterparts. Nevertheless, the government's Local Government Review in 1993 further eroded the power of local authorities, and the narrow constraining remit of the Banham Commission means that UK local authorities have difficulties in confronting the issues of the inherent weakness of subnational authorities, compared with other European states. UK local authorities see the challenge of the 1996 Intergovernmental Conference as an opportunity to argue for a stronger constitutional base for their activities. The existing treaty falls short, by confining subsidiarity to a debate between member states and the European Commission. Improving subsidiarity would mean incorporating the Charter of Local Government into a new treaty. The first step for a Labour Government would be to ensure that the UK is signed up to those principles espoused by the Council of Europe. The Committee of the Regions should have a democratic mandate as opposed to the current list of government appointees. It is particularly difficult to ensure the democratic accountability of a body where several of the locally elected members lost their seats at the May local elections yet continue to represent local regions in Brussels.

Without a doubt, an incoming Labour Government will have no shortage of policies to pursue both on the home front and in Europe. Regional development policy in Britain has been inadequate both in terms of infrastructure and investment. Expenditure on defence procurement has been higher than regional support. Eradicating the problem of poor housing, the decline in public services and poor transport networks will only be possible within the context of devolving power to the regions. Elsewhere in Europe, for example in Germany, regions are more successful and more competitive because they rely on a regional distribution of economic, financial and political power. The regeneration of Britain's regions will not be engineered by London or Brussels. It will only come about if those who have the interests of the regions at heart form strategic partnerships.

Building a new Europe which is responsive to citizens' needs and interests means building the right system of local government in the UK. The two objectives are mutually reinforcing. Labour has embarked on a consultation exercise in the regions, and through the newly formed Regional Commission will produce recommendations for democratic and economic regeneration. These proposals for the regions will make a critical difference to how UK local government operates in Europe. Strategic competencies, enhanced powers and partnership will be the prerequisites for promoting the principle of regional entrepreneurship, and creating key co-operative structures between employers, employees and local authorities. It is not only a question of ensuring, via strong regions, that the UK can get the best out of Europe, it is about involving citizens and encouraging them to participate in decision-making which affects their daily lives and giving them a say on regional differences and needs. This will also give us greater clout at negotiating tables in Europe and strengthen Britain's profile in the Committee of the Regions.

If Labour were to take office tomorrow, we could immediately make one small but immensely significant contribution to getting rid of the democratic deficit by democratizing the committees which distribute funds in our regions. We could replace the dead hand of government bureaucracy with independent bodies involving key partners in the regions. We could create a true sense of partnership, with a strong involvement by social partners. We could introduce flexible systems in local authority spending to allow grants to be taken up. We could extend automatic capital cover for ERDF grants to include the necessary 50% matching funds without making reductions in other areas of local authority finance. Such a change would remove the bureaucratic and abstract image of Europe and support inclusion, illustrating how Europe can strengthen and reinforce local and regional decision-making.

The Need for Democratic Cohesion

Economic and social cohesion has to be underpinned by policies which promote democratic cohesion. Britain in the late 1990s will have to make up for decades of regional neglect and economic decline. An increasingly pro-active policy in Europe will have profound social and cultural implications for Britain's regions. In government, Labour ministers will set about building strategic alliances with other member states to consolidate and defend the gains made in legislation which have led to the creation of a genuine economic, political and social community. Economic and social cohesion is a key component of a Europe built on solidarity. A Labour Government will need all its strength and political skills to maintain the commitment. A Tory opposition will lurch increasingly to the right, retreating into naked xenophobia and Little Englandism, and continuing to try to push British public opinion in an anti-European direction.

The real challenge for Labour will be to change our internal political climate to ensure that the electorate sees Europe not as an obstacle, stripping us of our national credentials, but as enabling and facilitating a higher standard of living for all. Part of the process of Europeanization and modernization will be to create a vibrant local and regional democracy. It has been said that people will begin to understand Europe when Europe has some significance for everyday life. It will be through effective local and regional structures that our citizens will be guided through the European maze. Only then will the benefits become clear.

Appendix 1
Structural Fund Allocations to the United Kingdom, 1994–1999

	Aims	Period Covered (calendar years)	UK allocation (£ million, 1994 prices)	UK allocation per year (£ million, 1994 prices)
Objective 1	promoting the development and structural adjustment of regions whose development is lagging behind	1994–99	1,860	310
Objective 2	converting the regions . . . seriously affected by industrial decline	1994–96	1,690	563
Objective 3	combating long-term unemployment and facilitating the integration into working life of young people and of young persons exposed to exclusion from the labour market	1994–96	1,240	413
Objective 4	facilitating the adaptation of workers . . . to industrial changes and to changes in production systems		-	-
Objective 5(a)	speeding up the adjustment of agricultural structures in the framework of the reform of the Common Agricultural Policy	1994–99	280	47
Objective 5(b)	facilitating the development and structural adjustment of rural areas	1994–99	640	107
Objective 6	promoting the development and structural adjustment of regions with an extremely low population density		-	-
TOTAL			5710	1440
Community Initiatives				
ADAPT	retraining of those whose jobs are at risk	1994–99	225	38
EMPLOYMENT	aids entry of disadvantaged groups into the labour market	1994–99	115	19
INTERREG	promotes cross-border co-operation	1994–99	86	14
KONVER	assists areas affected by decline in defence activity	1994–97	79	20
LEADER	promotes innovative development of rural areas	1994–99	51	9
PESCA	assists diversification of fishing ports	1994–99	29	5
RECHAR	assists conversion of coal areas	1994–97	127	32
RESIDER	assists conversion of steel areas	1994–97	35	9
RETEX	assists conversion of textile areas	1994–97	29	7
SMEs	assists small firms to adapt to single market	1994–99	53	9
URBAN	regeneration areas in cities	1994–99	77	13
TOTAL			906	175

Table taken from House of Commons, Trade and Industry Committee Fourth Report, Regional Policy HC356-I. HMSO, 29 March, 1995

Appendix 2
European Structural Funds: UK Objective 1 (1994–99), Objective 2 (1994–96 and Objective 5(b) (1994–99) Areas

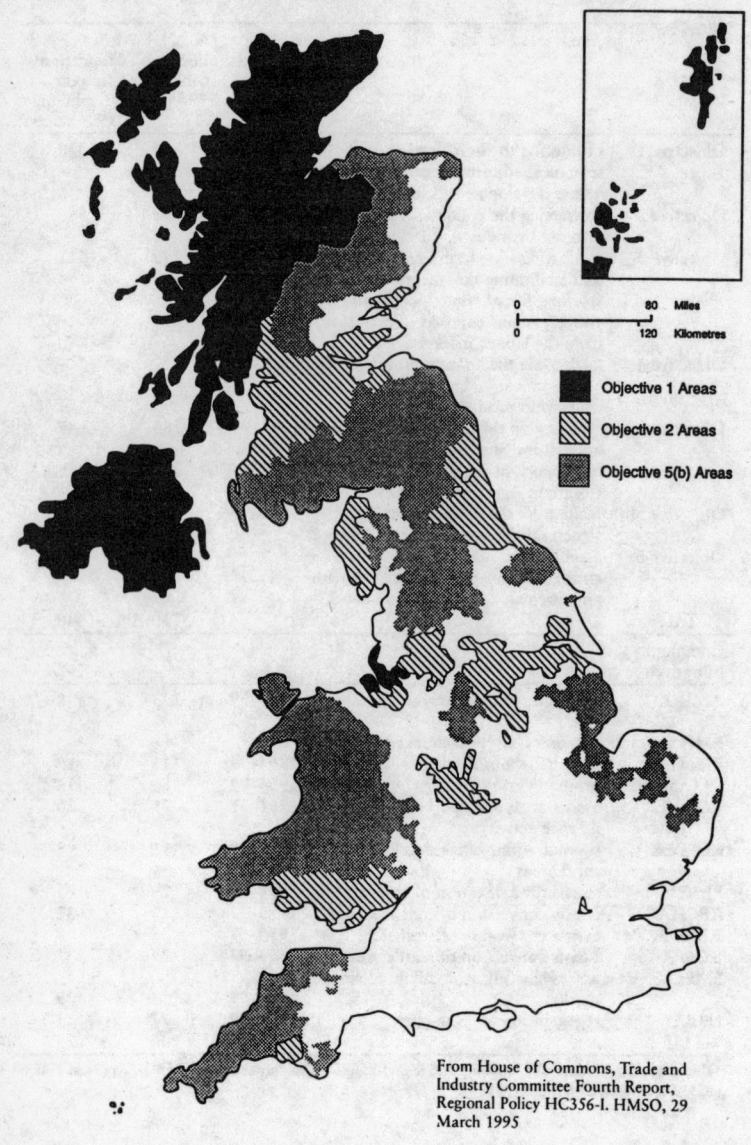

From House of Commons, Trade and Industry Committee Fourth Report, Regional Policy HC356-I. HMSO, 29 March 1995

CHRISTINE CRAWLEY
Women in Europe

For almost half a century, equality has been at the core of European integration. Since 1957, when reference was first made in the Treaty of Rome to equal pay for men and women (Article 119), the European Union has had a positive record of legislation and programmes to counter discrimination on grounds of gender.

Women have become increasingly visible in Europe's own institutions over the last fifty years. The appointment of five women Commissioners in 1995, and their election as 25% of the current European Parliament, demonstrates the progress Europe has made in promoting equal opportunities. Yet much remains to be done and we must be wary of thinking that the battle for equality is won.

This chapter, while concentrating mainly on the gender dimensions of European equality policy, also reflects on the European Union's continuing commitment to improving the life chances of all Europeans, through wider equal opportunities action.

It was my very good fortune to Chair the European Parliament's Women's Rights Committee for five years, from 1989 to 1994. The first part of this chapter is influenced by that experience and sets the context for the debate on women's roles in twenty-first century Europe.

A Short History of the European Equality Agenda

Almost all the gains made by working women in the United Kingdom over the past decade can be traced to changes in legislation at European level.

The British Labour Government of 1974 to 1979 found an ally and a persuader in the European Equality Agenda. The Conservative governments of 1979 onwards have, however, found European equality policy an irritant; an attitude which culminated in the infamous British opt-out of the Social Chapter.

Under Article 119 of the Treaty of Rome, a series of directives – legally binding laws which take precedence over national law – have been implemented. These directives have established a 'backbone' of equal opportunities law and rights in important areas: equal pay and treatment for women and men at work, in social security schemes, for self-employed people and protection of pregnant women at work.

The European Union has also issued a number of resolutions and recommendations, which, although not legally binding, address and promote issues of particular relevance to women. Resolutions and recommendations have been adopted concerning equal opportunities on education (1985), the integration and late reintegration of women in working life (1988), as well as recommendations on sexual harassment (1991), child care (1992) and women in decision making (1995).

Through the 1980s and 1990s, the Community has worked on promoting equal opportunities through its European Positive Action Programmes. These programmes are proposed by the European Commission, amended by the European Parliament and agreed by the member states. The four-year programmes have several aims: to support existing equality legislation and improve it, to finance women's vocational training projects; to promote the integration of women into the labour market; and to improve the status of women in society. The most successful programmes have been those where a limited number of priorities are targeted and where monitoring of member states' performance is taken seriously. In the European Parliament we are now calling for sanctions to be imposed on member states that ignore or inadequately implement European equality action programmes.

The Fourth Positive Action Programme (1996–2000), recently proposed by the Commission, recognizes the need for equal opportunities actions in *all* policy areas, an important concept for the future development of the equality agenda.

In addition to Community Action Programmes, a number of other funding programmes have been specifically targeted at women. Priority 4 of the European Social Fund's Objective 3 relates to 'promoting equal opportunities between women and men' and provides funding for vocational training and for child care while training. Other measures have included the new opportunities for women (NOW) programme (1991–1993), an innovative transnational training programme designed to help women find jobs; and the Local Employment Initiatives for women (LEI), grants which provide financial aid for the creation of women's businesses. Women have equal access to the new Socrates and Leonardo training and education programmes and can apply for funding from the HORIZON programme, which aims to improve the employment prospects of people with disabilities and other disadvantaged groups.

In addition, the European Commission funds an NGO, the European Women's Lobby whose role is to 'exert influence and put effective pressure on institutions in order to ensure that women's interests are more adequately defended and represented in the context of a more United Europe'. These umbrella organizations cover thousands of local women's groups, and ensure a grass-roots voice for women in Europe.

Issues for a future Labour government

A Labour Government must urgently address the morass of complex and ineffective bureaucracy that is delaying the payment of the European Structural Funds. Many women's training projects suffer delays, and women are often frustrated and bewildered by the cumbersome process involved, the length of time decisions take, and the difficulties involved in seeking transnational funding partners. Many argue that the funding arrangements have become too centralized and that delays in agreeing budgets have severely damaged many projects.

If European Funding is to play a significant part in enabling women to train, and retrain, for re-entry into the labour market, then a new Labour Government will have to persuade other member states – as well as its own electors – of the need to increase the budget in this vital area of European policy.

Women at Work – an Economic Force to be Reckoned with or an Underclass in the Workplace?

Being a working woman in Europe today is full of contradictions, burdens, opportunities, tensions, divided loyalties and struggle.

Vital statistics for European women today

- More women are working in the labour market than ever before, with a significant increase in the last ten years

- Before the year 2000, another 750,000 women in Britain are expected to enter employment
- By the year 2000, it is estimated that in Sweden the percentage of active working women will overtake that of men in the 24–54 age group
- Fewer women in Britain are presently working full-time than were in 1975
- British women are more likely to work part-time than women in most other European Union countries
- Women who are working have less free time than men in every EU country because of home demands that are not shared by male partners
- Women are joining Trade Unions faster than any other group
- Young European women under thirty years old are the best-educated generation of women ever in the history of the EU
- Increasing numbers of European women are involved in small business start-ups, as pointed out in the Delors White Paper

These factors have altered the structure of the labour market, of child care and of education and training, and have resulted in increasing numbers of women taking part in decision-making both in the workplace and in political and public arenas.

The Changing Labour Market

Seismic shifts have taken place in the European labour market. There has been a massive increase in women workers and a sharp decline in traditionally male manufacturing jobs. Forty per cent of the total working population in the European Community consists of women.

It is women who, along with other vulnerable groups –

such as young people and ethnic minorities – are most likely to take on low-paid, part-time and temporary work. European policies must recognize that while more women are economically active than ever before, their jobs frequently fail to provide them with economic stability or the opportunity to develop their skills to their full potential.

Training is one key to promoting women's opportunities in the workplace. The European Union has supported some innovative projects that combine the social interest of the worker with the economic objective of the employer, and encourage women's participation in setting their own goals, and identifying particular areas they see as discriminatory. Much remains to be done, both in extending the current levels of training courses targeted at women, and ensuring that all courses offered are geared towards women's needs. Gender-related factors such as holding courses at appropriate times, in accessible places with child care facilities, must be taken into account when courses are designed, if training is to be effective.

Issues for a future Labour government
The draft European directive on part-time and temporary work known as the 'Atypical Work Directive' should be examined favourably by a future Labour Government if the majority of women's work in the twenty-first century is to be more than low-tech skivvying. The directive would set European minimum standards for part-time workers, giving them the same pro rata rights as full-time workers, in terms of pay, training, pension rights, sick pay and holiday leave.

Equal Pay

The European equal pay legislation, in existence since the 1970s, has resulted in the gap between men's and women's pay narrowing in most sectors. Wages have shown little improvement in the lowest-paid areas of industry such as commerce, services and retail, however, which traditionally employ women. If we are to halt the growth of a two-tier society, it is imperative that a minimum wage is introduced, to protect the earnings of women and other vulnerable groups. The Labour Party recognizes this and a Labour Government has pledged that it will introduce a minimum wage.

The lack of progress in implementing European equal pay legislation, and the legal difficulties imposed on those women who wish to take an equal pay case to court, has led to the publication of a Memorandum on Equal Pay for Work of Equal Value. The memorandum argues that there is a need for clarification of the principle of equal pay for work of equal value, so that individuals may rely on it and national courts and tribunals may apply it satisfactorily.

A future Labour Government must apply itself to overhauling equal pay legislation. Its first step, as the memorandum suggests, could be to incorporate the following features into an equal pay strategy:

- Further research and studies into women and pay
- Improved legal training for lawyers and legal advice centres in equal pay cases
- A code of practice, in agreement with the Social Partners, explaining measures that can be adopted to address wage discrimination, i.e. revision of flat-rate pay, integrating grades and categories of gender-segregated workers, developing non-discriminatory job evaluation schemes and redefining educational qualifications.

Modern Men and Women Sharing Work at Home

When it comes to hard evidence of sharing work and home duties, the 'new man' is looking a bit old-hat. As Susan Faludi has said, 'The only major change in the last fifteen years is that now middle-class men *think* they do more around the house.' Women's time commitment to running a home is still substantially more than men's.

A recent survey by the Henley Centre shows that the average number of hours spent preparing food each week divides up between men and women as follows. In the UK, for every 8.17 hours a woman spent in 1991, a man spent 4.41 hours. In 1993 there was a tiny increase in men's participation, up to 4.72 hours, compared to 7.81 hours by women. While these statistics vary from country to country, the general trend is the same across Europe and shows that the equal sharing of food preparation, shopping and other household duties is a myth, as is the sharing of child care and caring duties for other dependants.

The European Union is currently bringing forward a directive which attempts to reconcile home and working life by concentrating on giving both parents a right in law to interrupt work to look after young children and dependent relatives, with up to three months' parental leave. As well as providing for parental leave, the European Union should be promoting public awareness campaigns on establishing a better balance between men's and women's sharing of work in the home.

Issues for a future Labour government

Britain's opt-out from the Social Chapter, negotiated by the Conservative Government, means that the Parental Leave Directive will not cover British families. It is therefore imperative for a new Labour Government to make opting back into the Social Chapter one of its first legislative tasks on gaining office.

Child Care

When it comes to caring for children, it is women who generally carry the major responsibility, and Britain in particular has lagged behind the rest of Europe in providing publicly funded child care. In Belgium and France, over 95% of children between three and five are in nursery education. In Britain, we lie near the bottom of any league table (only Portugal has a worse record), with only 40% of that age group receiving nursery education.

Lack of affordable child care is a huge barrier for mothers wishing to work, especially for single mothers. Britain is the member state with the largest number of single parent families – 17% of families with children under eighteen years, according to the 1992 European Commission Report on Lone Parent Families. Single parents in Britain are much less likely to be in work than in European countries where access to child care is better. In Denmark, 74% of lone parents are economically active, in France 68%, in Britain, the figure is only 40%.

Where women are not forced out of the labour market in their twenties and thirties to raise families, but instead stay in work with short maternity breaks, we see them adding to their skills bank and accumulating experience. They make their 'human capital' (the skills with which they trade) more attractive to the marketplace and their future work prospects are enhanced.

Where women take long breaks from the labour market, however, employers perceive their 'human capital' as of less value than men's. The persistent low pay of women has a great deal to do with this. In those countries where women do leave the labour market in their child-rearing years, they re-enter in their forties and fifties on much lower pay rates and with outdated skills.

It is no coincidence that in those European countries where public or government policy is geared towards structuring women's security in the labour market through the provision of support systems, the economy as a whole benefits. In Denmark, Sweden and France, where the growth rate is higher than that of Britain, public child-care policies are proof that supporting working women entails a healthy economy.

Issues for a future Labour government
The European Parliament has called for recognized minimum standards to be respected in access to child care across the European Community. The tardy response of Britain to this voluntary call confirms the need for a new European directive, mandatory for member states, in this area. A new Labour Government should pursue the development of such a directive as a major plank of its European policy platform.

Future European Action

The All-Party Women's Rights Committee of the European Parliament has a proud record over the last decade of promoting actions for equality between men and women. The committee led the European Parliament to amend the important Maternity Leave Directive of 1992, which resulted in improved maternity rights for thousands of British woman.

The European Parliament Women's Committee was also

a strong supporter of the European Commission in its recent campaign to persuade member states to adopt strategies to promote women's participation in political decision-making. We have seen the concrete results of this policy with women's membership of European institutions increasing substantially in 1995.

The European Parliament and Commission worked jointly in preparing the European Fourth Action Programme on Equal Opportunities (1996–2000). We emphasized the need for trade unions and employers to negotiate future lifelong learning courses, positively targeted at women, and especially women without qualifications. Lifelong learning is important if women are to become a strong force in the future information society, undoubtedly the key to tomorrow's working patterns. It is a worrying indication of women's marginalization in the information society that currently only one in seven users of the Internet are women. Prompted by the European Parliament's own research in this area, the Commission's Fourth Programme has proposed further research into the gender dimension of IT which will provide a basis for future Community action.

The European Parliament will be proposing a number of amendments to the Treaty of Union at the Intergovernmental Conference of 1996. Among these amendments will be the need, identified in my report, for a widening of the legal definition of the rights of women beyond the current definition of Article 119, which only refers to women's economic circumstances. Women continue to suffer from violence inside and outside the home and violence against women is a human-rights abuse – yet at present there is no legal base in the treaty under which to promote European action against violence towards women. Enshrining women's human rights in the treaty will not cause domestic violence to disappear overnight, but will bring the issue of women's rights to the fore and act as a basis for promoting European action.

At the Fourth World Women's UN Conference, the European Parliament welcomed the declaration that sexual and reproductive rights should be recognized as fundamental human rights. While this development is to be welcomed, there remains much to be done. A combination of Catholic and fundamentalist opposition blocked the demands of the European Parliament and other delegations that sexual orientation should also be included as a fundamental human right. However, the most important work is to ensure that the conference's results do not just remain a 'paper' declaration but are followed up and implemented through European and national policies.

Issues for a future Labour government
The next Labour Government needs to build on existing equal pay legislation and make sure it works in practice. Comprehensive child and elder support, social security rights, and quality training for women are our priorities, and decisive action will prevent women being the casual care labourers and digital drudges of the twenty-first century.

A Wider View of Equal Opportunities in the European Union

While this chapter has concentrated on equality between men and women, there are many other groups in society who have less than equal rights: the elderly, ethnic minorities, the disabled, and lesbians and homosexuals. At a European level, there have been several important initiatives to promote equal opportunities for these groups.

The European Parliament has consistently supported calls to extend the current treaty to include a declaration that no European citizen should be discriminated against on the grounds of a disability, their age, race or sexual orientation. The 1996 Intergovernmental Conference will provide an opportunity for European governments to prove their commitment to equality by adopting the European Parliament's declaration.

Issues for a future Labour government
A Labour Government needs to be clear about what it wants to achieve in equality policy at EU level. Whilst it is likely that a Conservative Government will take Britain into the 1996 treaty negotiations, it will, no doubt, be a Labour Government that will conclude those treaty negotiations in 1997. That new Labour Government must call for an end to what my colleague Stephen Hughes describes as the 'patchwork quilt of confusion' on the rights and guarantees afforded by the Treaty on Equal Opportunities, and it must set out a radical, achievable programme of legislation and action supported by the appropriate treaty changes. As the democratically elected representative of its peoples, the European Parliament has quite appropriately been at the forefront in promoting equal opportunities for all its citizens. Labour MEPs have played an important role in this process, and will continue to do all in their power to support equality at all levels and for all groups in Europe.

GLYN FORD
Racism, Residents and Refugees

The Treaty of Rome unequivocally requires the free movement of goods and services, capital and people within the European Union. The first three flow with enthusiasm; in the fourth case, blockages are found above and below the water. Yet people are the most crucial element if we are to construct a community rather than just a market. This freedom cannot be limited to member-state nationals; it must encompass all European Union residents. Otherwise we shall see the creation of a two-tier Europe.

On the continent, if *de jure* free movement is restricted, *de facto* free movement will be in force. In practice, travellers crossing the Luxembourg–French border by car already can do so at a speed exceeding the French speed limit. This kind of free movement means that third-country nationals will be drawn to economic 'hotspots' across member-state boundaries. There they will be illegal immigrants and hence exploited and drawn into a process of undermining hours of work, rates of pay and health and safety conditions. All this was graphically illustrated by the German investigative journalist Gunter Wallraff in his book *Lowest of the Low* (Methuen, 1988) when he described his experiences over twelve to eighteen months masquerading as a Turkish *gastarbeiter* (guest worker).

Racism, Residents and Refugees

The ultimate answer is for all residents of the Union to have the same rights and duties as everyone else. Problems have arisen in this area because initially the market-led Community paid little attention to social Europe. In the meantime the emerging new right occupied the political high ground with democratic parties throughout Europe at best abdicating their responsibilities and at worst leading low-race cards for the new right to trump. A deliberate confusion has been created between free movement, immigration and asylum issues and there is equivocation in tackling them head on.

Fascist Europe

As we approach the twenty-first century, a rising tide of racism and xenophobia can be seen sweeping across Europe. As far back as 1984 the European Parliament was sufficiently alarmed at the initial electoral successes of Jean-Marie Le Pen's *Front National* (FN) in France to set up a Parliamentary Committee of Inquiry into the Growth of Racism and Fascism in Europe.

The late Harold Wilson once said, 'A week is a long time in politics.' In contrast, the other face of political time sees five or ten years pass in a second. From extreme Right to new Right, they go from strength to strength. There are ebbs and flows, but the trend is upwards. The situation is worse this year than it was last and will decline further next year.

In Britain we have the British National Party (BNP), the National Front (or, as it's now called, the National Democratic Party), Combat 18, and the National Socialist Alliance acting as an umbrella under which these groups can jointly organize. In European terms, despite Derek Beackon's brief period as a BNP councillor in Tower

Hamlets, these parties are small beer. Currently, the real problems are on the Continent where the extreme right is an electoral force to be reckoned with. One measure of their success is their growing representation in the European Parliament over the past two decades (see Table 1).

Table 1: The extreme right in the European Parliament since 1979

	1979	1984	1989	1994
F		10	10	11
D			6	
I	5	4	5	13
B			1	3
GR	1	1		
A	Not in EU until 1995			5(1995)
UK		1		
TOTAL	6	16	22	32

In Belgium there are currently two Members from the Vlaams Blok and one from the Front National (Belge). Austria joined the Union on 1 January 1995. John Taylor of the Official Ulster Unionist Party (OUP) left the European People's Party (EPP). The OUP rejoined the EPP after the European Elections in June, 1989 when Jim Nicholson replaced John Taylor as the OUP Member.

Le Pen's politics can be summed up simply. He believes that the holocaust, the death of six million Jews and others, was 'a point of detail of history', and that the Americans built the gas chambers in Buchenwald after the war. Members of the FN have been convicted of arson, racial attacks, racial murders and bombings. In February 1995, a seventeen-year-old Frenchman from the Comoros Islands was shot dead in Marseilles. Three FN activists were responsible.

Earlier in the day, they had been putting up posters for Le Pen's presidential campaign. The leadership is slow to condemn and swift to deny. '*Agent provocateurs*' is normally their cry. Despite this, Le Pen's FN has turned itself from what was in 1983–1984 a refuge for protest votes, into a party that ten years on consistently gains the votes of between one in six and one in five Frenchmen and women. In the last presidential election (April 1995), the FN managed 6 million votes, peaking with 28 per cent in Saint Priest just outside Lyons, but with above 20 per cent in Alsace, Marseilles and Lyons itself. This neo-Nazi party cut with Poujadism has over 1000 local councillors who in a number of towns and villages, particularly in southern France, share power with those traditional right-wing parties whose members desecrate urban street architecture with stickers saying 'There are no enemies on the right'. Their strength was further boosted by local elections in June 1995 giving the FN outright control of the towns of Toulon, Orange, and Marignane.

In Germany, extreme right-wing violence continues on the streets and TV screens. Electoral representation in the European Parliament was lost in 1994 when Franz Schönhuber's *Die Republikaner* was split by the fission of Harold Neubauer's *Deutsche Liga*. Schonhuber was a wartime member of the Waffen-SS, while Neubauer was a former member of the NSDAP-AO, a right wing terrorist organization calling itself 'The German National Socialist Workers Party – Foreign and Development Section', based in the United States. The two parties, the *Republikaner* and the *Deutsche Liga*, exceeded the 5 per cent threshold necessary for election between them, but not separately. Thus parliamentary representation was lost because of internal, factional fighting rather than any substantial loss of electoral support.

In Belgium the Vlaams Blok has emerged as a racist and regional player on the political scene. Since 1994 they have had two representatives in the European Parliament, up from one in 1989. In Antwerp, they are the most popular single political party, only kept from power by a rainbow coalition stretching from Troskyists to Christian Democracy. In francophone Belgium the *Front National (Belge)*, using the French FN as its paradigm, won its first seat in the European Parliament in the last elections.

In Austria, Jorg Haider's *Freiheitliche Partei Österreichs* (FPO) grows at the expense of both the traditional left and even more the traditional right. The man who led the campaign to end positive-action measures to assist the Slovene-speaking minority in Austria's southern province of Carinthia, echoed revisionist views by saying in the Austrian Parliament that Hitler's employment policies were better than those of the governing coalition. He failed to condemn unequivocally those terrorists who booby-trapped a racist billboard so that it killed four travellers who tried to remove it. In the last general election (December, 1995) the FPO received 23 per cent of the vote. In the past, Le Pen, Schonhuber and Haider have met secretly together.

In Italy the *Movimento Sociale Italiano* (MSI), at the urging of its leader, Gianfranco Fini, has dissolved into the only marginally wider *Alleanza Nazionale* (AN). The AN was set up as a front organization to fight the Italian General Election of 1994 in a pact with Silvio Berlusconi's *Forza Italia*; neo-Fascists combined with embittered former Christian Democrats desperately seeking a home following the virtual annihilation of their former party by the Tangentopoli scandals. Despite the current post-Fascist rhetoric of Mr Fini, it was only months before the last election in March 1994 that he was promising to make common cause with Jean-Marie Le Pen's Group of the European right in their newsletter *Europe des Patries*. Not surprising, given that they shared a political group in the European Parliament during 1984–1989. The MSI only left when the *Die Republikaner* joined in 1989, because of the latter's revanchist views on the Italian Tyrol. It was only when other doors were opened that Fini closed the chapter on Le Pen. Not exactly something he would want to explain to the Royal Institute of Affairs (Fini addressed the Institute on 15 February, 1995).

Inquiring in Parliament

The report of the European Parliament's Committee of Inquiry came out in 1986. It was known as the Evrigenis Report, after its *rapporteur*, and labelled 'alarmist'. With the passage of time and in light of the above, it has turned out to be, if anything, over-complacent. It produced a string of recommendations, including proposals for a European Race Relations Directive, and the setting-up of a European Migrants Forum. But other than within the European Parliament itself, there was precious little evidence that these proposals were taken seriously. All that was achieved was a solemn declaration by the community institutions decrying racism and xenophobia (June 1986).

In November, 1989 a second and further Committee of Inquiry on Racism and Xenophobia was established, in response to the resurgence of the extreme right in the European Elections of 1989 (7 million votes and 22 seats), resulting nine months later in a report. This further report concentrated less on reiterating the conclusions of the first (which by then were becoming self-evident truths to students of European psephology), and more on identifying action to be taken, particularly the need for urgent legislative measures to protect Europe's 'Sixteenth State': the twelve to fourteen million third country nationals legally resident within the European Union and the four million black Europeans. This second report concluded with an overlong list, attributable to the European Parliament's working practices, of seventy-seven recommendations for action.

Committing the Commission

The European Parliamentary session subsequent to the two committees of inquiry has placed successive Social Affairs Commissioners Vasso Papandreou (PASOK, Greece, 1987–1993) and Padraig Flynn (Fianna Fail, Ireland, 1993) under considerable pressure to bring forward anti-racist legislation. Both have resisted the challenge, retreating into the arms of lawyers. The Commission has claimed it does not have a legal basis for action. Certainly the legal position has ambiguities, but it is a two-way street. The EC Treaty's social policy provisions, in particular Articles 117 and 118, alongside the declaration on fundamental human rights and the Solemn Declaration against Racism and Xenophobia signed by the Council, Commission, Parliament and member states in 1986 and now an addendum to the European Community treaties, offers a framework for action. The Solemn Declaration was used by Jacques Delors in 1987 to justify a subvention to the populist anti-racist youth group *SOS Racism* in France when questioned by the then Front National MEP Oliver d'Ormesson. Delors, then President of the European Commission, confirmed that initiatives and projects against racism were 'in line with the traditions and principles of human rights' and the granting of a subsidy to an anti-racism association like *SOS Racism* was also 'in line with the undertakings by the Community institutions' in the 1986 Solemn Declaration. With political will and backbone, even ambiguity can provide an opportunity. To paraphrase Gandhi, the Commission has had a problem for every solution.

Finally, however, Padraig Flynn moved and bowed to consistent pressure from the European Parliament, admitting 'partial competence'. In December, 1995 the European Commission adopted its first ever Communication on Racism, Xenophobia and Anti-Semitism, accompanied by a proposal to the European Council to designate 1997 as 'European Year Against Racism'. This represented a watershed after more than a decade's work.

The Communication sets out key areas for further action to be built into existing policy instruments. The key areas are grouped under seven headings:

- Promoting integration and opening pathways to inclusion
- Promoting equal opportunities and reducing discrimination
- Raising public awareness and combating prejudice
- Preventing racist behaviour and violence
- Monitoring and punishing racist crime
- International co-operation
- The question of European level legislation

The Communication also states the Commission's intention to press for a specific competence discrimination clause in appropriate Community legislation. On each and every one of these issues British reservations were expressed, uniquely amongst the fifteen.

Migrants Speaking for Themselves

The only area where the Commission acted upon the Committee of Inquiry's recommendation was, after much pressure, in respect of the European Migrants Forum (EMF). This proposal initially figured in the Evrigenis Report and was reinforced in the Ford Report. The Migrants Forum was modelled on the European Youth Forum, and intended as a representative body that would act as a sounding-board between Europe's 'Sixteenth State' and the Parliament, Commission and Council. The Forum has been up and running since 1991. However, it chose not to position itself in the niche it was intended to occupy between the Commission, Council and Parliament, instead diluting and, in effect, surrendering its special status by acting as yet another pressure group and not as the privileged body it was intended to be. This was partly because its members were appointed as individuals and not as *ex officio* representatives of their organizations, which would have made them accountable to their 'constituencies'. The Parliament has pejoratively noted this failure in its budget commentaries for 1994. The EMF had moved so far from its intended orbit that when the Council of Ministers set up the Consultative Committee on Racism and Xenophobia (of which more below), its existence had been forgotten.

More recently, as internal divisions have subsided, the EMF has started reorientating itself towards the Community institutions which were the initial intended target of its endeavour. If the EMF is to serve its 'Sixteenth State', it has a responsibility to direct and concentrate its efforts on the Community's institutions. But it must represent real people with real problems. Unless it does so, it should be killed off rather than suffering the slow death of increasing irrelevance.

Free Movement of Persons – Two Steps Forward, One Step Back

Following the specific recommendation of the second Committee of Inquiry in January 1992, the European Parliament established a Civil and Public Liberties Committee (renamed since July 1995 as the Civil Liberties and Internal Affairs Committee) and inaugurated an annual debate on racism and xenophobia.

A central area of concern to this new Committee was the failure of the Commission to promote the free movement of people with the same enthusiasm that it promoted the three other freedoms noted at the beginning of this chapter. Article 8A of the EEC Treaty states that 'the internal market shall comprise an area without internal frontiers in which the free movement of goods, persons, services and capital is ensured in accordance with the provisions of the Treaty'. The Legal Affairs Committee, responsible for this aspect of the Parliament's work, voted unanimously in October 1993 that legal proceedings should be brought against the Commission for failure to act. Almost two years on, with a European Court of Justice hearing looming, a New Commission was finally prodded into action.

The new European Commission, the first under the Maastricht procedure, took office in mid-January 1995. Within months Commissioner Monti, responsible for the internal market, announced two proposed directives on Free Movement to the Civil Liberties and Internal Affairs Committee. The key measures would abolish controls at internal frontiers, thus enabling member-state citizens and third-country nationals with either a residents' permit or valid visa for one country of the Union to travel within the Union without border formalities. The European Commission adopted the proposals in July 1995. Two steps forward, one step back: these new directives require unanimity in the Council of Ministers for adoption, and the first has a series of conditions attached which will almost certainly prevent it being implemented before the twenty-first century.

The British Conservative Government has been held hostage by Eurosceptics who portray free movement as a kind of illegal migrants' charter. This mentality was illustrated in February 1995 when Charles Wardle, then British Junior Trade Minister and a former Immigration Minister, resigned because Britain's internal frontier controls were in danger of being declared illegal by the European Court of Justice. Wardle fed the resulting tabloid frenzy with the idea that millions of immigrants were waiting inside the European Union, eager to decamp to Britain as the borders withered away. The whole imbroglio was put in context when even a leading member of the FN in Marseilles rubbished the claim, saying that he could conceive no good reason why a French-speaking Moroccan immigrant in France would want to move to the UK. Others put it more bluntly: who would want to move to the fifth-rising-fourth-poorest country in the EU and wait four years for a hip operation?

When President Santer announced the Commission's work programme for 1995, he was clearly mindful of the British Conservative Government's position, elaborately dressing up his poison pill in the language of Euro-scepticism. 'Citizens will not see the benefits of the frontier-free area unless the Union can demonstrate its capacity to guarantee their security and combat drugs traffic and organized crime. The Commission will make full use of its right of initiative wherever this is recognized in the Treaty. I am persuaded that there is no quality of life in society without security. That is why in matters of immigration and asylum, drug addiction and judicial co-operation in civil matters, where many citizens are likely to be affected, the Commission will seek to meet their expectations and allay their concerns.'

The only thing missing was rabies. But the sting was in the tail. In the actual text of the work programme, it is stated that dealing with the internal market implementation of Article 8A is the 'cornerstone of the Commission's activity'. Moreover, among the items under 'main initiatives and new legislative proposals' are free movement of persons; freedom to travel; practical elimination of border controls. While President Santer may have deliberately avoided overt confrontation with the UK government, the writing is on the wall.

A Multicultural Union

The European Union is in and of itself a complex multicultural community. Alongside the rainbow cultures of the fifteen states are the smaller communities from across Asia and Africa spread throughout the Union. Immigration has had a positive cultural and economic impact.

Already, more than twenty million out of the 370 million population of the European Union work in a state of which they are not in fact citizens. The large majority of these are the thirteen to fifteen million third-country nationals who are residents but not citizens. They are denied fundamental civil and political rights. Simple measures must be supported to extend the rights of this 'nation' which makes up Europe's seventh-largest 'state', falling behind only the big five of Germany, the UK, Italy, France and Spain, and placed between the Netherlands (with a population of just over 15 million) and Greece (with a shade over 10 million).

It should be made simple to acquire nationality after five years' unblemished residence in a country, and the children of immigrants born in a country of the Union should be granted automatic citizenship. Where necessary, the acquisition of dual nationality should be permitted. It is ludicrous that hundreds of thousands of people born and brought up in the EU, with no real ties with their parents' or grandparents' home country, and in some cases no knowledge of their language, are considered (as they are in Germany) to be foreign nationals. In France, with its new legislation, they are doomed to remain that way for the foreseeable future.

Consultative Commission on Racism and Xenophobia

If the Commission has been slow to grasp the nettle of racism and xenophobia, the Council has never tried. Since the establishment of the directly elected European Parliament in June, 1979, the European Council has for fifteen years limited its interventions to resolutions condemning racism, anti-Semitism and xenophobia after each new high-water mark tide of racial attacks, racial murders or anti-Semitic incidents. This pattern seemed finally to have been broken by the establishment of the Consultative Commission on Racism and Xenophobia. The RAXEN Commission, as it was referred to by the Council, was set up as a result of a Franco–German initiative launched at the Corfu Summit in July 1994 by Mitterrand and Kohl. The Commission under the chairmanship of Jean Kahn was composed of a representative from each member state, plus one representative from the European Commission, two from the European Parliament and an observer from the

Council of Europe. The initial terms of reference threatened to restrict its function. It was set up simply '... to make recommendations, geared as far as possible to national and local circumstances, on co-operation between governments and the various social bodies in favour of encouraging tolerance, understanding and harmony with foreigners'. While its initial report to the Essen Summit in December, 1994 kept within these constraining terms, the final report went much further in demanding action at a European level. This insubordinate report was presented to the European Council at Cannes in July 1995. It echoed all the European Parliament's demands of the previous decade.

These were, first, that during the 1996 Intergovernmental Conference (IGC,) a treaty amendment should be agreed to make it unambiguous that the European Community (an important distinction from the European Union) has competence to deal with the fight against racism and xenophobia. Second, for the European Commission to introduce a European race relations directive to make discrimination on the grounds of race or religion illegal for European Community residents. Third, that a directive should outlaw holocaust-denial and the distribution of racist and anti-Semitic material in written or electronic form. This would ban such video games (currently being passed around the playgrounds of Europe) as 'Concentration Camp Manager', where the player picks his victims – Jews, Pakistanis, Turks or Gypsies – and then has to manage his genocide by buying Zyclon gas with the money raised from the hair, gold teeth or jewellery of his victims to reach a winning total of six million. Fourth, to establish a European Observatory to monitor incidents of racism and xenophobia. Fifth, to ask that the European police and customs liaison organization, EUROPOL, take responsibility for exchanging information regarding neo-Nazi and neo-Fascist organizations, including those linked with football violence within the member states. Sixth, to recommend its own continuation until the requested treaty changes are ratified, whereupon the responsibility would shift to the appropriate Community institution with the enlargement of its terms of reference to include free movement.

At Cannes, the report's reception was overshadowed by a number of other events, including the Tory leadership contest and, more seriously, the deteriorating situation in the former Yugoslavia with an escalation of the Serb genocide of their Bosnian Muslim neighbours. Initial indications, including the draft Council conclusions and a promise from Felipe Gonzalez that the incoming Spanish presidency wanted to include anti-racism within its work programme, seemed to indicate the general acceptance of the RAXEN Commission's conclusions. However, the final outcome was that the Consultative Committee's mandate was merely renewed 'to study, in close co-operation with the Council of Europe, the feasibility of a European Monitoring Centre on Racism and Xenophobia'.

The term 'close co-operation' came under intense scrutiny as the Council of Europe attempted to hijack what was essentially a European Union initiative. To have anything more than close co-operation would draw the teeth of such a centre by a double dilution of its work: first by expanding its area of concerns to include the whole of the Council of Europe; secondly by making it a 'joint venture', with the Council of Europe placing inevitable limits on matching financial contributions. At Florence in June 1996 the principle of the observatory was accepted and the RAXEN committee asked to continue its work until the observatory was established.

Governments Alone and Together

Prior to Maastricht, competence for 'home affairs and interior matters' at a European Community level was consigned to the outer darkness of semi-clandestine inter-governmentalism: organizations like Trevi, the *ad hoc* group on immigration, the Rhodes group and the Schengen group, where the areas of responsibility were harmonization of policy in respect of combating terrorism, drugs-trafficking, prostitution, immigration and asylum. Schengen, in particular, continues to set Europe's agenda on these issues. These various groups, made up of EC interior and Home Office ministers and civil servants, on the basis of that 'liberal' agenda, treat Europe's migrant population as yet another generic problem alongside terrorists, drug traffickers and organized crime. The consequence has been the semi-covert ratcheting-up of repressive measures against immigrants and asylum-seekers by member states acting alone and in concert. They have been influenced by each others' fears to introduce more barriers to entry and fewer barriers to expulsion.

Frequently, asylum-seekers and refugees are subjected to inhuman treatment; held in the most primitive and repressive conditions in camps and hostels where the only way out is to withdraw one's asylum application. Deserters from former Yugoslavia's civil wars, who have fled after refusing to fight, have been shipped back by a number of EU States to face discrimination, violence and possible death. Portugal introduced a new immigration act in March 1993, allowing authorities to expel without the right of appeal foreigners not holding residence permits. On 26 May 1993, Germany abolished its constitutional right to automatic asylum.

In 1993, Edouard Balladur's French conservative government introduced measures to strengthen border controls, withdrew the automatic right for children of foreigners born in France to become French, and made it more difficult for French citizens to marry immigrants. Aspects of immigration law, which had been underpinned by the French constitution, were placed under threat. In the United Kingdom, the introduction of the 'habitual residence' rule has restricted the rights of EC citizens living in the UK. Changes in the social security legislation in April 1994 require EC citizens to have a 'genuine chance' of finding work in order to qualify for income support after six months. The Home Office will be informed and may arrange for income support to be withdrawn and declare the individual no longer lawfully resident. In November 1995 the Tories published their Immigration and Asylum Bill, a new high-tide mark in Tory attacks on asylum-seekers.

Nevertheless there is a two-way flow, with countervailing moves at a European level. The Spanish Presidency of the Council in December brought forward a joint action programme to combat racism and xenophobia with the aim of 'approximating' member states' laws and enhancing the opportunities for judicial assistance between member states in this area. The first time round, the package was rejected by the United Kingdom. The Home Secretary argued that Britain would not be lectured by the Europeans and that the UK already had adequate laws for dealing with racism. However four months on, under intense pressure and in the light of his request for member state co-operation to help combat hooliganism around Euro-96 via Europol, Michael Howard signed. But an annexe to the minutes stated that the UK will act as provided for in the joint action, 'taking into account the provisions and general principles of United Kingdom criminal law' and 'where relevant behaviour is threatening, abusive or insulting and is accompanied with the intention or is susceptible to incite racial hatred'. It would appear that even such a restrictive interpretation could necessitate changing UK legislation to at least allow prosecution, for example, of the further shores of holocaust denial in the form of *Holocaust News* or its ilk.

What Europe has is Asylum-Seekers

Despite the hype and activity, there is currently no primary immigration into the European Union, nor is there likely to be. What Europe has is asylum-seekers. All EU member states accept the 1951 Geneva Convention definition of a refugee. But through Schengen, Trevi and the rest, particularly since 1992, they have conspired separately and together to subvert the spirit of the convention to create a 'Fortress Europe'. The Carrier's Liability Act's fining of Airlines and Shipping Companies for bringing in individuals without proper papers turns check-in operators into the most hard-nosed immigration officers. Welcome moves towards a common visa policy are being used to extend visa requirements to new countries whose citizens just happen to have darker skins. The latest proposal is for one hundred and twenty-six countries to require visas by 1996. Asylum-seekers are being put into a 'one strike and you're out' situation. A failed application to one member state automatically triggers a stop in all others. Fair enough given a humane common asylum policy, but less so with the macho competition between Europe's Interior Ministers to demonstrate their lack of compassion. First point of entry rules means that a plane touching down en route to Europe or within Europe passes the problem to someone else, with victims of torture being shuttled around Europe's airports.

The bottom line is that refugee status can be refused to those who have a safe refuge anywhere within their own country or region. That accounts for former Yugoslavia. Equally vigorously plans have been made to speed up expulsions procedures for those judged not to meet the criteria for admission.

Schengenland

The Schengen Agreement was originally signed on 14 June 1985 by France, Germany and the Benelux countries. Italy joined them in November, 1990, and Spain and Portugal in June 1991. The past decade has seen a rapid development of the Schengen system, led by the five founding members. They have taken the lead in promoting a 'fast track' of European harmonization in these areas without the benefit of parliamentary scrutiny at either the national or European level. This inevitably creates a template in the best traditions of democratic centralism for future EU policy that will eventually bind the UK.

On 26 March 1995, the eight Schengen members – minus Italy, for technical reasons – opened up their internal union borders. Despite teething trouble, particularly in France with the incoming right-wing government of Jacques Chirac playing xenophobic politics, it worked and consequently *Schengenland* looks like becoming a permanent feature.

A computerized database with information on asylum-seekers who should not be admitted, illegal immigrants, and people with criminal records is in operation, with only limited data-protection regulations. Police can now operate across borders in 'hot pursuit' and issue surveillance requests on suspects in other countries. Within twelve months to two years, Britain and Ireland may be the only

EU member states outside the system. Ireland will not participate because to do so without the UK would mean the reintroduction of border controls between Eire and the North – a psychologically damaging blow to the peace process.

The European Parliament and Commission are excluded from the Schengen decision-making process. Schengen has filled the vacuum left by the Commission's failure to act. Thus Commission inaction, catalysed by Conservative intransigence, is allowing democratic ability to dribble away and Britain's longer-term interests to be ignored. Britain must participate in opening up the Union to the free movement of people. It is the only way to provide for the unique geographical position of the UK and Ireland within the Union. The directly elected Parliament is being squeezed out of the process by the failures and omissions of institutions prepared to tolerate the semi-clandestine procedures of intergovermentalism. The result is a loss of democracy and accountability.

This is compounded by a conspiracy of silence. Those who want free movement reach their ends through less desirable means, while those who want to retain frontier controls in the interest of maintaining the spectre of looming immigrant invasion are left with their xenophobia unruffled. What will happen when those Conservatives keen to widen Europe rapidly to the countries of Central and Eastern Europe – hoping to dilute social progress – realize this means admitting potentially millions of Czechs, Slovaks, Hungarians and Poles to the current Union?

The Left, Home and Away

Labour promised in its document prefiguring the 1992 British presidency that they would use the presidency, if they won the election, to inaugurate a European race relations directive. At the Party conference in October 1993, a text from Tony Blair's Home Office team was overwhelmingly carried. It stated, 'Action must be taken to combat the rising tide of racism, xenophobia and anti-Semitism, and Fascism sweeping across Europe. UK race equality legislation and enforcement – despite its weaknesses – remains in advance of the domestic legislation of other European Community member states. Labour will campaign within the EC for a specific race equality directive, applicable to all residents of the Community. This should provide protection against racial discrimination, harassment and violence. There should be a European Commissioner with a specific responsibility for race issues.'

The Congress of the Party of European Socialists on 6 November 1993 in Brussels adopted a manifesto for the European elections of 1994 in the presence of the then Party leader John Smith. This manifesto called for 'common European agreement applying to all external borders and territory of the European Union'; 'illegal employment and illegal immigration will be fought at a Community level'; 'integration should be made simpler for foreigners who have lived in the EU for several years, including the right to vote at local elections, family reunifications and simplified naturalization procedures'; 'extreme right-wing and racist activities must be prosecuted to the full extent of the law'.

Community Competence

There is a danger, with the single market, of creating a group of second-class citizens: European residents who are not citizens of member states, and member-state nationals who because of the colour of their skin are increasingly likely to be discriminated against. One only has to come through passport control at Brussels or Barcelona, Manchester or Milan to see the two-tier treatment already in operation.

Such policies of commission and omission coupled with rising racism and anti-Semitism have mutually reinforced each other. Tougher policies against immigrants 'prove' to the racists and their fellow travellers that they were right, 'There is a problem.' Rising racism allows 'public opinion' to legitimate the actions of reactionary governments. Consequently, violent youth feels racial violence is in order. There is an increasing rise in racist attacks on the Union's ethnic minority citizens and asylum-seekers.

The triple issues of immigration, asylum and racism are crucial to the future of the European ideal. If Community citizenship is to mean anything, it must entail the right to move freely within the Community and have equal protection in the different member states. But this cannot be limited to Community citizens. Under the present structure, decisions are taken and policy agreed by EU interior ministers under the third pillar of the Treaty of European Union. It is vital that the treaties are amended to give the European Commission unambiguous competence to take initiatives on race relations, including the power to propose a directive harmonizing race relations around the Union.

After the experience of the RAXEN Committee at Cannes, it is clear that there is a long way to go, yet a policy must be forthcoming, effective and accountable. Race relations must be brought within the first pillar (European Community) of the Maastricht Treaty and not remain in the third pillar (Co-operation in the fields of Justice and Home Affairs). This would make anti-discrimination on the grounds of race a common or basic principle of Community law, which would not be the case under the third pillar. Bringing race relations within the first pillar would enable the involvement of the European Court of Justice, so crucial in cases of sex discrimination, to arbitrate on these issues. The issue of sex discrimination is already dealt with under the first pillar, and there is absolutely no reason why race discrimination should not be dealt with in the same way. Sex-discrimination law within the European Union has a favourable knock-on effect in individual member states. Similar treatment for race would lead to a similar outcome.

The European Parliament has argued that the whole of the home and justice affairs pillar should be abolished in favour of the first pillar. From the point of view of accountability and democracy, it is difficult to argue otherwise. Both the Parliament and the Court of Justice would oversee all policy-making under the pillar.

It would be naïve to believe that treaty amendments alone could eliminate the racist menace and bring peace and harmony to communities divided by the issue of race and nation. Legislation, education and employment are all necessary but not sufficient conditions. Legislation to lay down clearly and police the limits of intolerance; education to ensure that future generations do not repeat the mistakes of the previous ones; employment to undercut the extreme right-wing slogan which, in the French version, intones 'Three million immigrants, three million unemployed, three million immigrants too many', with other national variants substituting appropriate numeric totals. The earliest example found is a chilling reminder of our past. A poster of the Austrian Nazi Party in the 1930s discovered by the Anne Frank Centre reads 'One million Jews, one million unemployed, one million Jews too many'.

The practical instruments of the Community institutions and legislation can be used to introduce a variety of measures which will begin to address the problems. Measures to prevent the entrenchment of a 'Sixteenth State' of disadvantaged migrant workers who bear the brunt of European economic and racial antagonism; guarantees of equal rights for all in a single market, allowing non-EC nationals already legally resident in a member state the same rights of free movement as European citizens, with a goal of 'same rights, same duties for all European Union residents'; the introduction of a positive policy to combat racism and xenophobia at the European level, and humane and civilized policies on visas, refugees and asylum-seekers. All of these send a clear signal to the forces of the new and extreme right that European Union governments are committed to the fight against racism and intolerance.

In the United Kingdom, there is nothing to fear from the removal of frontiers and the free movement of people around the European Union. The United Kingdom will not be flooded with immigrants if our external frontiers to other member states are removed. Since 1993 we have in fact witnessed a decline in the number of immigrants entering the European Union. Our own anti-racist legislation embodied in the Race Relations Act leads Europe and shows how much is to be done. Progress at a European level, led by a new Labour Government, can be a symbol of hope, not fear. We will find that a rising tide of tolerance and prosperity will float all ships.[1]

---

[1] I would like to thank Sarah Chilton for her help with research on this chapter.

GLENYS KINNOCK, MEP
Development Perspectives and the EU: Combating Poverty in the Global Village

> *Our common humanity transcends the oceans and all national boundaries ... Let it never be asked of any of us – what did we do when we knew that another was oppressed?*
>
> Nelson Mandela, President of South Africa

We are continually reminded of the interdependence of our world and, since the end of the Cold War, there has been unparalleled globalization of communications, investment, trade, and production.

Yet as the world seemingly gets smaller, so the gap between rich and poor gets bigger. The challenges we face are common to us all. They have to be tackled with common solutions and common action and with relationships which are based upon respect and mutual growth.

Some of the dangers we face from radioactive emissions, for instance, are obvious. Other dangers, less dramatic, more insidious and cumulatively just as lethal, threaten life and the means of life. Acid rain in the industrialized countries, rapacious exploitation of land and minerals by commercial interests and overfarming by the desperately poor in developing countries simultaneously poison and punish our planet. If we cannot now make the strong moral case for change, for partnerships with the poor, then surely self-interest dictates that we should work to eradicate the scourge of poverty.

The rise of religious fundamentalism, the growth of the narcotics trade, the spread of AIDS and environmental degradation are just a few of the issues which concern us in the north of the world and which flourish in the poverty of the south. The European Union must join the battle against global poverty – against shortfalls in health, education and housing – and the powerlessness which the denial of these basic human rights brings with it.

In Mozambique over 90% of the people live in poverty, in Nicaragua six out of every ten people are unemployed and 73% live in poverty. How do you define poverty? A former President of the World Bank has defined absolute poverty as 'a condition of life so limited by malnutrition, illiteracy, disease, squalid surroundings, high infant mortality, and low life expectancy as to be beneath any reasonable definition of human decency'. I say it means going to bed hungry every night.

Women in southern countries, who work from dawn to dusk for little or no recognition or reward, are disproportionately represented amongst the poorest people. The December 1995 European Council meeting did agree a very welcome comprehensive resolution on gender and development. The resolution acknowledges association between the measures necessary to promote and protect women's social, economic, political, cultural and sexual rights and EU development practice. It is essential that policies promoting and protecting the rights of women in developing countries should not be peripheral, or exist in isolation, but should inspire and inform all aspects of policy. Only then can we ensure overall coherence.

It is necessary to focus on the need not only to create

growth but to ensure its benefits are shared more equally. The responsibility for working for such change lies largely with the industrialized world which controls and determines trade and market access, prices for the commodities on which so many southern countries depend, and debt alleviation.

The Debt Crisis

The debt crisis is growing. The debt of the poorest countries in Africa has tripled, with disastrous effects. It drains Africa of the resources it needs for investment in health and education. The vicious circle of poverty, ignorance and death turns again.

The North receives billions more from the South in repayment than it gives in aid. When Euro Disney recently suffered a setback of two billion in debt, their banks agreed to cancel eighteen months' interest payments and forget repayment for three years. Yet Uganda, one of the poorest countries, still pays over half its yearly export earnings on servicing its debt.

There are thirty-two severely indebted, low-income countries, and sub-Saharan Africa accounts for twenty-five of them. If we look at Uganda's social indicators, we see the grim facts behind the statistics. Infant mortality rates are 113 per 1000 live births. Uganda's death rate is twice the average for low-income countries. Children are dying of chest infections, diarrhoea, and malnutrition, and per capita spending on debt repayment is more than double per capita spending on health. How can such a position be justified?

The World Bank is making some progress on debt relief for impoverished debtors. In the Socialist Group of the

European Parliament, we shall be pressing for more comprehensive debt relief. When we give programme assistance, we should pay more attention to the nature and the commitment of a government to its people – not whether it is prepared to commit its country to what may be an alien ideology. We should look for allies among other European member state donors who will support our view that the independent countries should have the autonomy they were once promised restored.

EU governments can make an enormous difference and should use their leverage with banks and institutions to have debts cancelled. Neither the World Bank nor the OECD say anything different about the group of low-income countries which have the most debt. As the OECD baldly puts it, 'debt obligations, even after restructuring, are still beyond their ability to pay'. Unfortunately, the EU also lacks resolve. The EU should use its weight in a co-ordinated way in the international fora when debt is under review.

In particular, the EU should back Britain's proposal for the IMF to sell off its gold stocks, invest the proceeds, and use the resulting revenue to subsidize repayments to the IMF. If the EU were to accept this proposal, it would make a difference. The stock of debt owed to the institutions has more than quadrupled since 1982 to reach $49 billion. The IMF and the World Bank absorb an increasing share of repayments, leaving poor countries with no capacity to service their bilateral debt.

A recognition in 1990 that most ACP countries face severe debt problems has not led to any new serious initiatives to cancel loans made under previous Lomé Conventions. The Lomé Convention concluded between the Community and African, Caribbean and Pacific countries (the 'ACP Group') is the world's first comprehensive aid and trade agreement. Here again, however, the debt problem is simply not being treated. We need an integrated approach for reducing debt with the IMF and the World Bank, but also a better response from the European Community. Actions speak louder than words.

Development Aid

It is of course the case that three-quarters of the world's wealth is to be found in the industrialized nations and too often their actions are governed by narrow self-interest. Such indifference to misery, suffering and waste should shame and galvanize us all.

The furious row concerning the European Development Fund for the African, Caribbean and Pacific states, including the states of Southern Africa, is not just another spat about money. We are well and truly into the 'beyond Lomé' debate. As parliamentarians, we need to engage in this debate and not allow discussions to take place in secret, behind closed doors. It is especially important that ACP countries should be directly and effectively involved. We should see future negotiations as an opportunity to revitalize and review the Lomé arrangements. Colonial guilt is no longer a feature of European responses to the South, and European priorities have shifted in favour of Eastern and Central Europe, and the Maghreb countries.

It seems the EU wants spending priorities to be reflected in the Lomé partnership, and a reallocation of certain responsibilities. The whole issue of trade preferences will also need to be addressed because of the Single European Market and global trade liberalization.

The Maastricht momentum with regard to Lomé has not been significant, and the EU development priorities need to be restated and reasserted. The views of new member states who have less sympathy with the Lomé partnerships, based upon what they perceive to be colonial history, are an additional factor which will also need to be taken into account.

The Lomé review, and the EDF decision within this, was originally envisaged as a relatively low-key stocktaking exercise, but has become the battleground for a larger and growing conflict over the future shape of the aid and development policy of the European Union and its member states.

The post-Lomé debate has also highlighted a more widespread phenomenon of aid-donor fatigue. In February the OECD reported that after two decades of stability in the real value of world aid, there had been a marked fall to $59 billion in 1995 – the latest year for which figures are available. The organization saw no sign of a likely upturn in the following years. Global aid is now at its lowest level since the recession-hit 1970s.

The fall in official aid has come just as private capital flows to the south have slowed markedly – most of these flows are, in any case, concentrated on a relatively small number of better-off countries in East Asia and Latin America.

More recent signs do not augur well either. The United States have agreed a reduction of over $8000 million in aid to Africa over the next two years. With the Cold War rationale gone, the Republican Congress had been proposing more or less to wind up large chunks of the American aid programme as part of its publicity-grabbing crusade on government spending and its attempts to usurp the foreign policy powers of the President. Jesse Helms, chairman of the Foreign Relations Committee, described development aid as 'pouring money down a rat-hole'.

Such open hostility towards aid is not displayed by decision-makers on this side of the Atlantic. However, with over 18 million people now out of work across Europe and the economic recovery slow and faltering, support for the views of the extreme right has grown and, along with it, the xenophobic message that 'charity begins at home'. Certainly, the aid budgets of a number of European countries have suffered a severe drubbing recently.

The EDF/Lomé crisis had brought out of the shadows the marked shift in, on the one hand, the EU's geographical priorities, and, on the other, its attitude to both its foreign and security policy and its aid and trade policy. The ACP share of the EU market has fallen to under 4% – a drop of 50% since the fist Lomé agreement was signed two decades ago. It is therefore necessary to adopt a constructive and innovative approach to EU relations with ACP countries. A long-term development perspective is needed, and they should be fully involved in negotiating new partnership agreements with the EU.

If one takes a comprehensive look at EU aid as a whole, simple donor fatigue is not enough to account for the proposed curtailment of funding for the ACP countries through the EDF. Over the next five years, the total EU foreign assistance budget is set to be over 27 billion ECU, nearly twice the amount originally proposed, but rejected, for the EDF. The money is there – it's a question of where it is being sent.

The facts belie the claims that member states cannot afford to give to the EDF – or that they are resisting too much of their aid going through Brussels. Total EU aid has tripled over the last decade but the EDF share of the total has shrunk sharply, especially in recent years. In 1990 the EDF made up over half of total EU aid. Just three years later it had already shrunk to a third. Some of the growth in the total is accounted for by funds going to Asia and Latin America. Most of it is due to the rapid expansion of programmes for Eastern Europe, the former Soviet Union and the southern Mediterranean – set to rise threefold by the end of the decade over 1990 levels.

Agreed at the Edinburgh Summit in 1992, the near-doubling of the ceiling for the EU's external affairs budget was not articulated at the time as an explicit shift in priorities. But that is what it represented. Given the unwillingness of governments to increase overall aid budgets, the present squeeze on EDF funds for Africa is the corollary of the increase in aid to those regions deemed to have a new and higher priority. This is not to dispute the importance of action to support, say, Eastern and Central Europe through its difficult economic transition. But this cannot and must not be at the expense of the poorest countries reliant on aid support, most notably in Africa.

When all is said and done, it is a question of political priorities and the signs are that Europe is downgrading its commitment to Africa. Few people in Europe realize this and – judging by what evidence of public opinions on aid exist – few would support this threat to sell the poorest nations short.

In response to this change, some would point out that there need not be such a trade-off: if member states were prepared to increase the size of their programmes to allow for aid being channelled through Europe in line with the new commitments, then Peter would not have to be robbed to pay Paul. But some are pointedly not prepared to do so, others are reluctant. The EDF debate therefore falls in the thick of the tussle between those member states who want a minimalist approach to aid delivered through Europe, with the emphasis on preserving their own bilateral programmes; and those whose emphasis is the reverse, with central Commission-run programmes more pronounced.

The issue is not subject to any clear written ruling as to whether aid policy in pursuit of the development goals spelt out in the Maastricht Treaty falls within the primary competence of the Commission or the member states. It is fudged in the treaty, which says only that the common European development policy should be 'complementary to the policies pursued by the member states'.

To make the issue even more fraught, these tensions over development policy also reflect the highly sensitive splits over the role of the Community versus the member states within the not yet properly established Common Foreign and Security Policy, of which development co-operation is destined to be a part.

Finally, Lomé is under pressure not only in its aid component – but on trade too. In the firing-line have been the trade preferences granted to the ACP countries and protocols covering certain key products and countries.

The long-running banana drama has crystallized key elements of the debate. Under Lomé, the EU is committed to buy a certain quota of bananas from ACP producers, most notably the small island states of the Caribbean. Here, bananas are the mainstay of the economy and the thousands of small farmers who grow them. Despite increasing markets in Europe for the so-called 'dollar bananas' grown largely on Latin America plantations, the Lomé deal came under attack from both member states and GATT. There was a head-on clash with those who would not countenance the use of special trade allowances for poorer countries as a ladder out of poverty. Lomé trade preferences and other trade schemes have been increasingly scorned as outdated, with the prescription of blanket trade liberalization held up as the only answer.

It is in my view important that we resist any diminution

of the support provided by the Lomé banana regime. The Caribbean growers simply cannot afford any further weakening of the support they receive, particularly through any additional increase in the tariff quota, for dollar bananas.

All these points of concern within the current EDF/Lomé debate are themselves a product of some more fundamental issues now facing European development policy – and indeed, that of all European member states.

The Case for Aid

One challenge is from those who say simply: 'aid isn't working'. The traditionally conceived package of aid projects and programmes is seen as having failed to achieve the aim proclaimed for it: the defeat of global poverty. At one level, there is no disputing such a conclusion. This failure has occurred in a world with more than enough wealth and know-how to end absolute poverty within a generation; a world in which the gap between rich and poor is widening, not narrowing. A world where, according to the UNDP, in 1960 the richest fifth of mankind had thirty times more wealth than the poorest fifth; but where they now have sixty times more.

Reducing Poverty

Poverty is the world's biggest killer. About 1.3 billion people live in absolute poverty. The average life expectancy for people living in the North is 76 years. In the developing world, life expectancy is 50. In the North, 6 out of every 1000 children born die before their fifth birthday. In the south is it 320 out of every 1000 that die – just under one third. First-year death rates for babies in the South are even worse. A baby born in Africa, for instance, is fifteen times more likely to die before its first birthday than a baby in Europe.

As this makes clear, nowhere are the running wounds of poverty more obvious than in Africa. Not only has progress here been too slow, it has been put into reverse. Slumped commodity prices, soaring debt, stagnant aid flows and economic mismanagement have taken their toll across the continent. Africans are, on average, a fifth poorer today than they were a decade ago, according to the World Bank. The hard-won gains of previous decades – against illiteracy, avoidable child deaths and malnutrition – have been eroded.

The stubborn persistence of many of the profound problems of poverty, underdevelopment and humanitarian crisis has led some to write off the whole idea of aid. This is wrong for two, very different reasons. First, it ignores the success stories of development – the economic development and real progress in human welfare that have been made in many countries, especially in Asia – and the supporting role aid has played. Countries like South Korea that are now becoming aid givers, were once major recipients themselves. Nearer to home too, the kick-start of Marshall Plan aid helped war-ravaged Europe get back on its feet. Those who write off aid altogether too easily forget these examples. Second, it is a misjudgment to condemn aid for failing to banish poverty, because so little aid has in fact been targeted on this task. It has, instead, been serving commercial or political aims.

Despite the renewed upsurge in rhetoric about poverty reduction in recent years, the UN reckons only 6% of aid from a country like Britain is actually focused on providing basic needs – like clean water and basic health care – to which taxpayers generally believe aid should be targeted. So rather than rejecting aid out of hand we should be taking a critical look at how little aid is doing what we are told it should: tackling poverty.

As we approach the twenty-first century, over a billion people still live in absolute poverty. This is not only the greatest human tragedy; the fact that it is preventable makes it the greatest political challenge we now face. In the seconds it takes to read this sentence, a child will have died from easily preventable causes. We must re-engage with these challenges through the twists and turns of the debate over the shape of European development policy. We must not lose sight of the realities behind the statistics or the implications of a policy based on cynical self-interest.

Even if colonial ties contributed the original rationale, Lomé's focus on many of the world's poorest countries must be preserved as the central tenet. Europe must maintain an expanding commitment to the countries where the worst problems of poverty exist. If the Maastricht pledge that Europe is in the vanguard of the campaign against world poverty is to take effect, it has to consist of more than words.

This is one of the greatest arguments in defence of preserving the ACP group, many of whom share common patterns of very low-income, commodity-dependent economies. That being said, there could be closer coherence within EU programmes to 'least developed countries' outside the ACP group, such as Bangladesh. Some new member states with respected development policy track records – such as Sweden – have mooted such ideas.

In addition, the poverty-focus of the EU's programmes must be developed and strengthened. Well-established programmes on areas such as rural and agricultural development should be built on and improved. Focusing on poverty-reduction must, however, take into account some of the global shifts in international foreign and security policy.

Promoting Security

One such shift is the ending of the Cold War. I use the present tense deliberately. In the aftermath of the fall of the Berlin Wall many western policymakers have still not adapted to the reality that their central assumption in international affairs for half a century has undergone a seismic change. Across the globe, this transformation has released external constraints on movements to peace and stability in deeply entrenched conflicts from Namibia to Cambodia.

Faced with such upheaval, policymakers in European capitals have too often eschewed imaginative leaps. Instead, they have clung to the familiar and the short-term. The reaction has often been a short-sighted and limited one, with the same old arms-based approaches to security being carried forward and a host of new enemies being identified in the south.

This concept was well summed up by the CIA chief appearing before Congress when he said: 'We have slain the dragon, but live in a jungle full of snakes.' Snakes, it seems, that need to be put down by force – whether in the shape of the illegal drugs trade or fundamentalism.

Western governments still admonish Third World countries for spending too much on the military, while eagerly backing their arms exporters to sell as much expensive and sophisticated military equipment now markets at home have reduced. The five permanent members of the UN 'Security' Council manufacture 85% of the world's arms and two-thirds are sold to the developing world.

Despite pledges given after the fall of the Berlin Wall, aid and development efforts have been diverted from the Third World to the former Eastern Bloc – and the many promises by Western leaders that any such assistance would be *additional* to aid to developing countries have been quietly forgotten.

While the notion of the peace dividend as an instant cheque was always misplaced, there are very hard decisions to be made about what will in fact give the best value-for-money in promoting genuine long-term security: the development that tackles the poverty and inequality at the root of so many conflicts, or the military force which can be used to contain the symptoms of conflict once it has erupted.

The end of the Cold War should enable us fundamentally to rethink our approach to security – something that the EU should address in approaching the debate about the Common Foreign and Security Policy. Promoting development should be recognized as a key part of promoting security – common security, real security.

Helping an Andean farmer to grow alternative crops to coca, the raw material for cocaine, which can be sold for a price above rock-bottom international prices of crops like coffee, is likely to achieve more than the weaponry and military muscle the West has poured into the Andean countries to try (unsuccessfully) to stamp out coca production by force. Europe should be boldly investing in such initiatives if we truly want a safer world for our children.

World Trade

Less sudden and dramatic than the toppling of the Berlin Wall, there is nevertheless a huge economic shift with potential for the same scale of global impact: the rapid advance of economic globalization. This goes beyond the simple growth of trade, which has been occurring for centuries. It is a quantum leap in the global interlinking not just of countries, but of economic production itself.

Trade has grown faster in absolute terms over the last couple of decades than ever before. It has grown faster than overall economic output and is a sure sign of the internationalization of production. About a fifth of the twenty trillion dollars world output is now traded; twenty-five years ago it was only an eighth. Everything, it seems, is 'trade-related' today, from what films Europeans see in their cinemas to what seeds Indian farmers are allowed to plant in their fields.

The range of what is traded has widened. Services now account for nearly a quarter of all trade. Communications and information technology – from the Internet to dramatically cheaper international phone calls – are stimulating many new forms of economic activity and making knowledge-based services tradable via phone lines and computer disks.

The nature of trade is changing too. The traditional arms-length exchange of goods between different companies in different countries is no longer the key dynamic. More and more trade is between different parts of the same global corporation or through joint ventures. Half of US trade is estimated to be of this kind; as much as four-fifths of Britain's.

Central to this process is the growth and development of the transnational company, which has dramatically changed the nature of world trade and production. As competition between these companies escalates, they no longer plan their production, distribution and financing on a national or regional basis, but on a global one. These corporations account for perhaps a quarter of all production in the world's economies. Of the world's 100 biggest economic units, half are countries, half are transnational companies. As a world, we are bound more closely together economically than ever before.

This does not mean, however, that one can jump from the economic reality of greater globalization to dewy-eyed notions of the market forming one world. Because while we are all becoming more closely linked economically, differentiation and inequality may grow wider.

In part, this will take the form of some movement towards a more multi-polar world economy. The dominance of the developed market economies clustered round the G7 countries is still clear. They control half the world's manufactured trade. However, the rise of Southeast Asia is undeniable. The process of globalization seems to be occurring through a new triad of economic power – North America, Europe and Southeast Asia. Each has a developing regional trade base from which they launch trade and investment forays into each other's territory.

Many countries outside these blocs fear being shut out in the cold – most notably South Asia, Africa and Latin America. In all these regions, the world of regional trading blocs is acting as a spur to redouble efforts to breathe life into regional economic initiatives – through the particular model such initiatives seek to follow is itself a crucial debate with which the EU should constructively engage.

This has profound implications for politicians and decision-makers who are still largely nationally based. For many politicians, including some on the left, economic globalization is an unpalatable truth which they would prefer to ignore. They recite old formulations of national-based solutions which are doomed to failure in today's global economy. Or under slogans of 'charity begins at home', they seek to withdraw into economic isolation and old-fashioned protectionism. Equally, there are those who simply throw up their hands and say there is little that can be done to direct or shape the globalization of markets; that we can do little more than go with the world market flow, perhaps just trying to ameliorate life for those who are most hurt in the process.

I reject both these forms of fatalism. The rapid shift in the reach and power of international companies seems to me to be one of the central reasons fro the need for democratically accountable structures which match the cross-border reach of the corporate giants. And I believe there is also a vital role for the EU to play on the global stage, raising not only its own narrow trade interests, but being prepared to take account of the trade needs of developing countries. In particular, the EU should be ensuring that the new World Trade Organization sees its role as broader than simply opening markets.

The effects of trade decisions on incomes, jobs and the environment must be considered more fully. Most crucially, the EU must ensure that the WTO explicitly addresses the trade needs of developing countries, especially the poorest. It should be prepared to grapple with reviving key commodity agreements, such as that on coffee. It should also urgently address the need to allow space for some form of trade preference scheme within the context of the normal multilateral rules on trade. We must ensure that agreements such as Lomé, which seek to reclaim a little from the injustice of the global trading system, are not ruled out of order by the only real world trade court we have.

The Poverty War

More people have died over the last forty-five years due to our unfair, unchecked and unbalanced economic system than during the First and Second World Wars combined. There is a world war today, and it is one that claims the lives of more than 12 million children under the age of five each year. Eighty per cent of those children would survive if given treatment costing 13p or less.

We cannot escape the fact that poverty is a man-made disease that scars the whole of our planet. It is an economic disorder requiring political solution at a global level. As one economist put it, at the moment we have a system that 'understands price but not value, money but not worth, fiscal but not moral rectitude, and financial but not social cost'.

Poverty is something we *can* afford to cure. It is something we *cannot* afford to ignore. It breeds disease, ignorance, inequality, instability, intolerance, privation, division and war. If the West sets a high premium on the elimination of these elements, then we must prioritize a twin strategy to promote poverty eradication and sustainable development. It is the South that most needs the first, and the North that most needs the second. They both need each other.

Poverty isn't simply bad for our conscience, it is bad for our business. We cannot sell high-value products to one-fifth of the world's population that currently languish in extreme poverty. As companies band together in the shape of multinational corporations to hunt for new markets, political organizations must follow suit in order to reclaim sovereignty from untrammelled market power.

The facts tell us that markets prioritize arms shipments above polio vaccinations. It is the responsibility of politicians to reverse this. The EU, given its history and the unique example it represents of regional governance, has a particular responsibility to change the status quo.

At present, Europe is part of the problem, not the solution. The EDF wrangling over contributions is just one example of the intransigence and short-sightedness which characterize our attitude towards aid and development. Our contribution, here in Britain, in Europe and in the North as a whole, *must* be bigger; not only in monetary terms, but in terms of the political will and inventiveness we give to the cause of combating poverty in our global village.

CAROLE TONGUE
European Media and Cultural Policy

The cinematic dream
On 13 February 1895 the first moving film strip was patented by Louis and August Lumière. These moving images created a sensation. When, in 1905, the novelist Leo Tolstoy saw a silent film of himself sitting in his porch, he was so excited that he declared, 'It is no longer necessary to invent stories. Just go about filming people in their day-to-day lives.' For Tolstoy, the moving picture was both a cultural artefact and a mirror of society, fulfilling by the power of images the story-telling role of the novelist.

The passion and power of film-making in Europe was fully developed in the 1930s by great artists such as Jean Renoir, Joris Ivens and Robert Flaherty. Films like *Une parti de campagne*, *Borinage* and *Man of Aran*[1] did reflect on humanity – on beauty, as well as on the raw struggle for existence by mankind – and essentially fulfilled that original vision of Tolstoy's as he screened those early moving images. This is an important memory to cherish. The power of film, and now also of television, to reflect its society, as a

---
[1] *Une parti de campagne*, Jean Renoir, filmed in 1936, France.
Borinage, Joris Ivens, Belgium, 1933.
Man of Aran, Robert Flaherty, Great Britain, 1934.

story-telling medium that can transport an individual through time and across continents to other cultures, has not diminished.

As we celebrate the centenary of cinema, we recognize with bitter irony that the hopes and dreams of the Lumière brothers, the vision of Leo Tolstoy, and the passion of Renoir, Ivens and Flaherty have been devoured and consumed by an electronic revolution fuelled by profit alone. It is worth remembering that in the past small art cinemas and film societies distributed the work of eminent film makers. The means and cost of production were modest. The film makers, each an individual auteur, could create their films successfully in Sweden, Spain, Italy and France for a wide European audience, transcending language and cultural differences, to celebrate what we now call 'pluralism' and 'diversity'. Mega, global, multinational corporations now own and control the means of production and the means of distribution. The dreams, with few exceptions, have been lost. It is our task, within a Europe-wide Parliament, to build a programme of economic support for European filmmakers, for development, production and distribution, in order to retrieve that dream.

The European institutions have recently adopted the Media 2 programme. This programme will give 310 million ecus over five years to assist training, film development, distribution and European film exhibition in cinemas. We now need to introduce further measures of regulation that ensure European culture and identity can not only survive, but will be celebrated in the millenium.

The Audio-Visual Industry

Concentration

The electronic revolution in the audio-visual industry can be characterized by three major trends: concentration, commercialization and globalization. It will not be long before we shall be able to receive hundreds of channels on our television screens. Boundaries between traditional broadcasting and the world of telecommunications will blur as broadcasting and point-to-point services are transmitted along the same cable, and as telephone and cable companies increasingly come to provide broadcasting services.

We know how politically powerful media concentration can be. We must have some means of control if our screens are to continue to reflect the cultures of Europe. Cross-ownership of press, media and telecommunications companies will create dangerous monopolies, making it almost impossible for newcomers to enter the market. Most of our European companies are minnows by comparison to Sony, Disney and Microsoft. With take-overs, the smaller companies would disappear into the stomachs of the global sharks. The key issue for Europe's media is how to maintain real diversity and a plurality of provision while at the same time building an indigenous European industry, powerful enough to resist the US-owned giant media corporations.

In very recent history we have seen the media's immense power to influence political choices. In Italy, former Prime Minister Berlusconi controlled 45% of television airtime, and used the channels he owned to promote his political party; in the United Kingdom, the *Sun* newspaper declared on the morning after the 1993 General Election, 'It's the *Sun* wot won it!' The political class is still anxious to neutralize the effects of Rupert Murdoch's ownership of both BSkyB and 37% of UK newspaper circulation: such cross-ownership confers real political power.

The independence of the media, freedom of speech and information and the protection of privacy all affect the kind of democracy in which we live. Broadcasting must enrich our democracy rather than distort and corrupt it.

If we fail to regulate now, we shall have:

- even greater media concentration threatening diversity of information and opinion
- unchecked concentrations in press-ownership threatening independent sources of information, editorial independence and journalists' freedom
- commercialized programming of game-shows, sensationalist and violent tabloid television, advertising and shopping dominating our media

Commercialization

Broadcasting is increasingly influenced by market forces rather than by any formal obligations to uphold the public interest. Sadly, 'we are the first generation since the war to hand on a broadcasting system with a narrower range of imaginative possibilities than we inherited; we've got a multiplicity of channels all saying the same thing and signifying very little.'[2] It is vital to continue with the best of national public service radio and television systems and channels with a public service mandate throughout Europe. *They* are the broadcasters who can best deliver diversity and pluralism through a wide choice of programmes and spread of opinions. All broadcasters, whether public or commercial, must continue to broadcast and produce high quality programmes and live up to the reputation British broadcasting enjoys for creative quality, technical excel-

[2] Alan Plater, 'People's Showdown', *New Statesman and Society*, 16 June 1995, p. 25

lence and genuine diversity, which has been built on a public service ethos throughout the system.

Public service broadcasting and public service obligations are currently the only means of ensuring a multiplicity of independent sources of information. Public service broadcasting answers to a different set of criteria than simple profit maximization. It is freed from short-term concerns about maximizing audience ratings and can therefore be a true innovator in programme-making, enriching the culture of the nation. The programme obligations placed on the UK broadcasters, the BBC, ITV and Channel 4 are positive, requiring quality and diversity across a wide range of programming. In addition, the United Kingdom broadcasters provide critical funding to underwrite feature film production. British television is a clear leader in its support for the film industry: in the last three years all British Oscar nominations have been for projects mainly dependent on television funding.

Above all, public service broadcasting is the only way to ensure that all our voices are heard and all our stories are told. The alternative has been described by Anne Applebaum:

> Imagine an enormous 18-lane superhighway, decked out with every modern computerized convenience. Now imagine that on this enormous, 18-lane superhighway, the only cars are ancient 1950s models, Edsels and Chevrolets, cars with fins and multiple headlights. Satellite TV is like that: the best, the newest, the most exciting technology, the herald of a new information age – and nothing to see except American series, old and new, American game-shows, old and new, American talk-shows and American-style talk-shows, American films and endless sports.[3]

[3] Anne Applebaum, 'Welcome to Mr Murdoch's world', *The Spectator*, 3 December 1994, p. 34.

This is already happening. In Europe there is a growing reliance on American programming due to commercial pressures, their cost advantage – one-tenth of the price of UK programmes – and the desire to maximize profits without investment in original programmes.

This has contributed in part to the European Union's trade deficit with the United States in the audio-visual market, which is now $3.7 billion a year. Colossal though this is, the figure conceals the true extent of the imbalance. The US earned $4.1 billion from its trade with Europe in 1993 whilst the EU earned only $336 million in the US.

One of the principal reasons for this US domination of world audio-visual markets lies in the fact that American producers recoup production costs within the United States. Therefore, any overseas income represents net profit. In the past fifteen years, the proportion of US-made films in European cinemas has grown from 35% to 80%, while today European films account for only 1% of the US market. In addition, North American interests control European film distribution networks: 85% of cinemas in the United Kingdom, as well as the control of satellite and cable TV companies broadcasting in Europe.

Many assume that the audio-visual industry is 'just a business', like any other. But television and films are not like cars or carrots. These sources of powerful images are the means by which cultural values are transmitted in modern society. Together with newspapers and publishing, they are a mirror for social and political life. Images of our own community, be they from *Spender* or *Eastenders*, are indispensable in enhancing our self-respect and self-esteem, and play a vital part in ensuring social cohesion, stability and well-being.

Globalization

In 1995 a report commissioned by the Writers' Guild of America predicted that by the end of the century the world's media could be controlled by just four organizations.[4] Some have responded to this trend by arguing for huge European multimedia giants to compete with North-American Japanese interests, unhampered by complex legislation, maintaining that only big players can survive in the big market. But this view of the future fails to understand what is really at stake.

Michael D. Higgins, the Irish Minister for the Arts, Culture and the Gaeltacht, has identified the key question:

> Why should all the images of the planet be produced predominantly from one space, as one expression of culture, at one period of time, in one narrow straitjacket? Clearly there must be choice from a cultural point of view and healthy competition from the economic point of view . . .
>
> We are talking about the right to make the case for films and television programmes to be made that will upset us, and jog us and startle us and technically do things with colour and image which have only been scratched yet. But instead of it being technology-driven for the narrow and exclusive interest of commercial investment, that its craft, and its art and its liberating power, be protected within cultures, so that film then is a tool of cultural diversity within a democractic definition of culture.[5]

What our audio-visual industry must do is create film and television that reinforces our European identity and culture,

---

[4] Alan Plater, 'People's Showdown', *New Statesman and Society*, 16 June 1995, p. 25.
[5] Extract from an interview with Michael D. Higgins: Midge Mackenzie, 'Renaissance Man', in *Broadcast*, 9 December 1994.

preserving our sense of particularism and distinctiveness. We should use the new technologies to our advantage. The massive expansion in bandwidth, the number of channels, the possibilities of truly local programming, the possibilities in education and information programmes, the falling costs of re-visioning material and of producing CDs and soundtracks encoded in up to ten languages on each disc – all these things mean that the audio-visual industries should be seen as a key means of *developing* a European cultural identity, not just shoring up what is already there.

Future Developments

Programming models

The ARTE cable channel is a very positive example of what is needed. It shows principally European documentaries, film, drama and magazine programmes made by Europeans. It is broadcast in French and German and is the fruit of great political will by Chancellor Kohl and the late President Mitterrand to engage in real cultural collaboration between the two countries. The channel was set up in the teeth of opposition but is now firmly established and expanding to include Switzerland, Spain, Sweden and beyond in the near future. Britain should of course be part of this exciting cultural partnership and contribute our Scottish, Irish and English cultural output to ARTE, if we are to develop a truly European Public Service Broadcast system.

Another television project which should command public and private support is Mondial, which seeks to create a new global satellite and cable channel offering a new range of choice for audiences through broadcasting films and programmes made in Europe and the world, and to enhance the range of diversity of quality television. New television channels like ARTE and Mondial are absolutely essential if the full extent of Europe's cultural creativity is to appear on the screen for our delight and education.

With the advent of new digital terrestrial channels, there are huge new opportunities for the UK's wealth of talented programme-makers, many of whose work at present rarely reaches the screens. The government should ensure that sufficient resources are available for investment in indigenous programmes for these new channels. This could entail allocating some of the franchise money paid to the Exchequer to programme-makers. This will require a long-term approach; investment now will bring economic and cultural dividends later.

Employment

The film and television industries are a significant source of high-quality, skilled employment in the United Kingdom, with 222,000 people currently employed. The fact that industry analysts are projecting that traditional manufacturing will fall to 2% of our work-force within the next twenty-five years underscores the urgency with which we must act to ensure our full participation in the audio-visual industry.[6]

More than ten years ago, Jacques Delors, former President of the European Commission, stressed the cultural and economic importance of the media in a speech to the European Parliament:

> The culture industry will tomorrow be one of the
> biggest industries, a creator of wealth and jobs. Under
> the terms of the Treaty, we do not have the resources to

[6] Jeremy Rifkin, 'The End of Work', *New Statesman and Society*, 9 June 1995, p. 18.

implement a cultural policy; but we are going to try to tackle it along economic lines. It is not simply a question of television programmes. We have to build a powerful European culture industry that will enable us to be in control of both the medium and its content, maintaining our standards of civilization and encouraging the creative people among us.[7]

Regulation

During the 1980s, European media policy focused mainly on the economic aspects of media, because culture, as Delors said, was not mentioned in the original treaties. Possibilities of action have been limited in the past. However, the Treaty of Maastricht of 1992 introduced for the first time a section on culture and specifically mentioned audio-visual policy. This is a welcome first step. Anti-monopoly laws or other measures to promote pluralism and diversity in the media are, however, currently ruled out by the terms of the legal framework within which the European institutions operate. The PES will demand changes to the Maastricht Treaty, including a commitment to promoting media and cultural pluralism and audience access to high quality public service television.

Most governments agree that it is now virtually impossible for individual nations to decide autonomously on many key policy areas. This is certainly the case for audio-visual policy. This is why we now need to build even stronger links between our own front-bench in the United Kingdom, and our members in the European Parliament to ensure their participation in European policy and legislation at every stage of this debate.

[7] Quoted in Richard Collins, 'Unity and Diversity? The European Single Market in Broadcasting and Audio-Visual, 1982–93', *Journal of Common Market Studies*, Vol 32, No 1, March 1994, p. 90.

Central to the debate on the audio-visual industry is the question of programming regulation, to encourage and ensure the production of European-made programmes, and whether this can best be achieved through programming or investment quotas.

Quotas have been challenged on the grounds that they are 'protectionist' and 'defensive'. I rather see quotas as shorthand for preferential treatment for European productions or legislation for a minimum of European content in programming. Quotas are not a new idea. Very early on in the history of cinema, the US government recognized that the audio-visual industry had enormous cultural and economic power, and successive US governments have, over many years, fiercely promoted their audio-visual industry through quotas and finance regulations (Finsyn/Prime Time Access). Canada also has indigenous programming and investment quotas on cable and public channels, which has proved successful and profitable. Within Europe, several countries already have quotas. The Netherlands has 40% Dutch programmes and the UK itself has very strict obligations for the BBC, ITV and Channel 4. A minimum 65% UK content is the rule. For the BBC, home-grown production stands at 85%; for ITV and Channel 4, 65% of programmes have to be originally produced or commissioned by them.

The UK is luckier than most of our continental neighbours. Our history of public service broadcasting, alongside wise regulation, has enhanced the local content of our channels. The BBC invests an enormous £1.2 billion in its own programmes and produces some of the highest quality in the world. I strongly believe that this level of investment has to be replicated by public broadcasters throughout the European Union.

The present European Television Without Frontiers

directive aims to ensure that 51% of programmes on our television screens are European. The European Commission proposes in a revised directive to eliminate the phrase 'wherever practicable', to strengthen European programme content and to make it legally enforceable. This law should be further strengthened with investment quotas: a mix of quotas is necessary to allow a breathing-space for European industry to restructure, and for investment in indigenous creative programming to be stimulated.

Broadcasting needs a constant pressure towards high quality. European media policy can be designed to create a thriving European programme industry with European catalogues of films and television programmes, which would give us a degree of control over what we can access in the cinema and on television in a digital age. This is not protectionism. It is about creating the space for European film-makers to make great drama and documentary films that will be shown widely. It is about building a strong and competitive audio-visual industry in Europe which should offer at least a million new skilled jobs in Europe by the end of this century. It's about exploring our own cultural identity, exchanging our own ideas, understanding our own lives.

A framework of laws

On the one hand, our media needs to be internationally competitive and yet on the other hand we must balance this with the need for diversity and pluralism which is so crucial in a democracy. The European Union should not solely confine itself to ensuring a free market of capital, goods and services. The far more important freedom is one which will offer the genuine free movement of people and ideas across frontiers. This is the challenge before us.

The PES in the European Parliament wants a framework

of laws to ensure that public interest and democracy are enhanced. They can be summarized briefly as follows :

- Television Without Frontiers directive to provide for fair and progressive programming and investment quotas for all channels
- MEDIA 2 programme and a European Guarantee Fund for film to support our European audio-visual industry and strengthen our production base
- Enhancement of public service broadcasting. We must ensure that public broadcasters are properly supported, properly sustained and properly funded
- European channels like ARTE and Mondial to be supported by public and private finance
- A European directive on media concentration
- European Freedom of Information Act
- Support for European multimedia software and a European programme to promote the development of CD-ROMs exploring Europe's history and culture.
- European television standards directive to be continually revised to ensure equal access to all service providers on digital television
- Universal access to information from local, national and European institutions and free access in libraries, schools and community centres to such information, as well as to a wide range of educational and entertainment CD-ROMs.
- New protection for intellectual property, enhancing authors' and creators' rights
- New privacy laws

Further to European Union action supporting indigenous film and broadcasting, the European Union has developed other cultural programmes.

Kaleidoscope is a programme which supports and promotes artistic and cultural activities: in particular, projects, seminars and meetings, and training courses. This programme has been running for five years and will be extended for a further three years. A wide range of projects are funded, from youth orchestra tours in Europe, to baroque art exhibitions in several capitals, to theatre training days, bringing together artists from all over Europe.

Ariane is a new programme which aims to promote books and reading through support for their translation into other languages. This will enable some of Europe's most rich and colourful poems, plays and dramas to be read by many more Europeans in their own mother tongue. At present, this programme is blocked due to UK government opposition. This is outrageous. The programme must go ahead.

Raphael is the newest programme in the cultural field. It will provide support for Europe's architectural heritage. It will possibly be used for big projects such as the Tower of Pisa or the Acropolis but also for other smaller projects; for example, the restoration of the Shakespearean Globe theatre in London.

Finally, the Socrates programme is the European Union's educational programme which provides funding for schools, universities and teachers to profit from study in another European country. Such opportunities offer young people a chance to explore other cultures, broaden their knowledge, their horizons, increase learning and communication, and facilitate exchanges of experiences and ideas across Europe.

These programmes deserve the continued support of governments and should be strengthened in the future, because they allow common European cultural projects to be developed, enhancing our common heritage, which we all delight in, and helping people to explore their own cultural identity, exchange ideas and understand their own lives and the lives of fellow Europeans.

Cultural democracy

Europe has millions of creative voices crying out to be heard and countless exciting and illuminating stories to be told. We must ensure that those voices find expression.

Culture is the foundation of socialism. It is the recognition of the other. For many on the right, culture is just a commercial product. We, as Socialists, agree we want to preserve and enhance existing cultures, to give everyone knowledge and access to cultures outside their own; and support new forms of culture. We are committed to this. Enhancing human communication and understanding enriches us all.

John Casey has written:

> To say that we are culturally European is not to refuse respect for diversity. It is only through being Europeans that we understand the cultures of China, India and Egypt. Eurocentrism is a necessary condition of our being citizens of the world.[8]

As Socialists, we wish to open up decision-making to allow active citizens to take part and ensure all voices find expression. To do this, we must overcome the ideology of the pure free-market. Government must intervene, create rules and invest in creativity. Above all, we must give all our young people a chance to enjoy real cultural freedom; to learn about their own continent and beyond, and to travel, live and study in other countries. That is the surest way to individual fulfilment and cultural democracy.[9]

---

[8] John Casey, 'There's a lot more to being British than being British', *Daily Telegraph*, 20 July 1995, p. 16.

[9] I would like to thank Professor James Curran, Professor Andrew Graham, Midge Mackenzie and Louise Tinkler for their helpful comments and advice on the writing of this chapter.

MARK F. WATTS
Going Places: A European Transport Vision

Transport has now become one of the major political issues of the 1990s. The pressure of more people demanding mobility, locally, nationally and internationally, has thrown transport systems into chaos. The resultant increase in car dependency is choking Europe's cities; it ruins the air we breathe and creates stultifying congestion that threatens total gridlock. The UK government's initial answer to this crisis was to build more roads. This policy has now been exposed as misplaced and out of touch. The challenge that confronts the left in Europe is to develop an alternative transport strategy to address the environmental implications of transport infrastructures as well as economic implications for the movement of goods and people.

Grass-roots popular protest has been a major catalyst in changing the emphasis in the transport debate, especially in the UK. The environmental movement has begun to widen its focus from anti-road to anti-car action. Car dependence has excluded whole sections of society from the transport system by the cost of travel, inaccessibility of services, or inability to use a car. A new, exciting transport debate has started, questioning the means of local, national and international mobility. The role of the car in society is at the heart of this debate. It is within this context that the

European Union has embarked upon a common European transport programme.

The European Union is rightly promoting the free movement of people across the borders of member states, as enshrined in the Maastricht Treaty. To facilitate such free movement, the necessary transport infrastructure must be available. In 1992 the Commission produced a White Paper, 'The Future Development of the Common Transport Policy: a global approach to the construction of a Community framework for sustainable mobility'. The trans-European transport network represents the major part of this framework and has been promoted by the Commission as the big European vision for the future of transport. An exploration of the implications of such a network forms a large part of this chapter, which also examines some of the smaller-scale ideas Europe is producing to deal with the problems of transportation for the twenty-first century.

Safety

Three crucial questions must be asked of any proposal to develop transport policy initiatives: is it environmentally sound; is accessibility maximized; is it safe? Although this chapter concentrates on the environmental and accessibility issues of transport policy, safety is an overarching consideration. The stark facts make this clear. Fifty thousand lives are lost and 1.5 million people are injured in the European Union every year in transport accidents. On Britain's roads alone, over 4,000 lives are lost every year and over 50,000 people are seriously injured. Large-scale single disasters in every mode of transport have been too common in recent years throughout Europe. There have been the ferry tragedies involving the *Estonia*, with the loss of over 900 lives in September 1994, and the *Herald of Free Enterprise*, with the loss of 193 in March 1987. Air travel has had the Schipol disaster in The Netherlands. Rail crashes like that at Clapham Junction are too frequent across Europe; while the daily toll of car pile-ups, especially those involving coaches, on Europe's roads exceeds them all. Accidents can be prevented. The European Union can lead the way by applying preventative legislation and enforcing it *before* disaster strikes rather than after. Strict legislation from Brussels could alleviate the appalling record of transport deaths, rather than leaving safety measures to the national level where they are failing with fatal consequences.

The European Parliament has led the drive to improve safety in the European Union. In June 1995 the Parliament ensured that new legislation to force 'roll-on roll-off' ferries to abide by a strict safety code will become law. The regulations drawn up by the International Maritime Organization will take effect in July 1996 in EU countries. The issue of seat-belts is another area where the EU is responding to pressure from the European Parliament. New legislation will ensure the compulsory fitting of seat-belts in all minibuses and coaches.

Britain's Roads

The current state of UK transport patterns is dramatically revealed in a study by John Adams from the University of Leeds, which records trends in travel in Britain since 1952 and looks at Department of Transport forecasts to the year 2025. Adams shows that while travel by bicycle has declined by 80% and bus by 50% over the last thirty years, car travel has increased tenfold and air travel thirtyfold. Rail travel has remained constant in passenger miles, but geographical accessibility has shrunk with line and station closures. Adams sums up the way transport has developed in the UK: 'The democratic and environmentally benign modes of transport are in retreat and the élitist and environmentally damaging modes are in the ascendant.'

Despite this, the Tory Government spends £3 on roads for every £1 spent on public transport and only 26% of the Department of Transport's budget was allocated to public transport in 1994. In 1989 the government launched its much-vaunted national road-building programme. The UK was to be restructured around a vast and comprehensive motorway network. Many A-roads were to be rebuilt as expressways, with a rash of towns and cities ringed by their own miniature M25s and brand-new routes supposedly opening up rural areas to development.

That road programme is now in disarray. It has been damaged by a combination of a popular grass-roots protest movement, opposition from other government departments and a series of damning official reports. The Royal Commission on Environmental Pollution recommended that planned expenditure on motorways and other trunk-roads should be reduced to half its present level and the resources released should be used to expand less environmentally damaging forms of transport. This was only one of 110 recommendations, many of which were directly in conflict with the Government's existing transport policy. The Standing Advisory Committee on Trunk-Road Assessment (SACTRA) report also struck at the heart of the Government's ideology. SACTRA, a body appointed by the Secretary of State for Transport, had the task of responding to claims by environmentalists that new roads generate traffic. The SACTRA report confirmed the 'so called' traffic-inducing phenomenon. The implications for transport planners of an official report concluding that new roads generate traffic are considerable. There is a powerful argument in favour of urgent investment in alternatives to reduce congestion. As SACTRA confirms, building by-passes to cure bottlenecks simply encourages greater amounts of traffic onto the roads with the bottlenecks just moving elsewhere.

The UK Government is seven years into what has been called the most ambitious road-building programme since Roman times. It is now confronted with official reports that say new roads generate traffic and increased traffic levels seriously damage our health and environment.

The Lessons for Europe

The lessons for Europe are clear. Just as roads will not solve the chronic transport problems of the UK, neither will they solve the problems of Europe's transport infrastructures. The Royal Commission Report on Environmental Pollution gave a succinct appraisal of the direction of European transport policy, stating that 'the Community's legislative record of environmental achievements in the transport field is not encouraging', but pointing out in mitigation, 'more progress has been made in creating an integrated European Transport policy in the past five years than in the previous thirty'.

In Europe, until recently, transport policy has been viewed merely in terms of facilitating the movement of goods and services to underpin the functioning of the single economic market. Environmental considerations have been either neglected or added only as an afterthought. Pollution does not respect national borders, and since the fastest-growing source of that pollution is the transport sector, environmental concerns must be at the heart of a common European transport policy.

Trans-European Transport Networks (TENS)

Under Commissioner Neil Kinnock, European transport policy is dominated by one scheme: TENS, an enormous project originally launched in the Commission White Paper of July 1992.

The TENS project is for the development of a modern road, rail, air and waterway system, with the objective of providing the EU with an efficient transport system. Its original aims were to integrate cities, link peripheral regions and underpin the development of the single market, thereby facilitating job creation both in its construction and its consequences. Neil Kinnock has called this the development of the Transport Single Market. The vision is of a Europe linked by multimodal transport networks with integrated transport-operating systems.

It is envisaged that by the year 2010 the European Union will be linked by 65,000 km of high-quality roads and 70,000 km of rail, of which 23,000 km will be high-speed rail links. In addition there will be 12,000 km of inland waterway.

The project is based on national transport plans. The member states are expected to find most of the finance themselves, with only a limited contribution of about 10% of the project cost coming from the EU. The Commission have estimated that the total cost will be 400 billion ecu up to the year 2010. At present, TENS exists as a series of routes drawn on maps weaving across Europe. It is an ambitious attempt to link the peripheral parts of Europe with the core, and a significant move away from the *laissez faire* approach to transport policy that has been prevalent in the UK. It is a big European idea.

Socialists must be supportive of this comprehensive attempt to plan transport systems. Employment is the key European issue for the next few years. The transport sector is itself a big employer and TENS will boost employment in other sectors. The best transport infrastructures in the world, such as Japan's, have been developed by a process of long-term planning and central funding. Market forces and fragmented networks do not produce comprehensive and integrated transport systems that serve the people's needs. The Republicans in the USA have recognized this. In the UK, the CBI has consistently advocated transport planning.

TENS will also provide the necessary framework for the harmonization and standardization (interoperability) of European transport, on the basis that quality of service will be raised throughout Europe to the level of the country with the best record in transport provision. In essence, the TENS project is a symbol of the fact that many of Europe's major transport problems can only be solved at the European level.

Despite the welcome return to a vision of planned transport provision, the TENS programme has come in for heavy criticism, especially from environmentalists. Environmental considerations were not even mentioned in the original terms of reference for the Christopherson Group, the working-group that prepared the TENS programme. Equally, the majority of the preparatory work on TENS involved road planners and members of the road lobby.

This domination of the planning stages of the TENS project by the road lobby has had serious implications for the development and legislative progress of the proposals. One of the most alarming contradictions with European environmental policy concerns carbon dioxide emissions. According to some provisional estimates, TENS will give rise to additional carbon dioxide emissions, leading to a probable overall increase of 60% in the transport sector by the year 2010. However, the European Union is committed to stabilizing carbon dioxide emissions at the 1990 level by the year 2000, and then subsequently reducing emissions. At present, the EU is unlikely to reach this target and the advent of TENS threatens to jeopardize commitments designed to protect against climate change.

The approach by the European Union had been one of reverse evaluation. It had decided on a plan of action in the transport field without consulting environmental experts or assessing the likely consequences. Evaluation and safeguards have come only after the legislative process has been set in motion. There is still uncertainty over the economic benefits of the project, since no economic assessment has been undertaken.

The TENS programme can be put back on track. The European Parliament has led the campaign to 'green' TENS in an effort to make up for the shortcomings and flaws built into the original proposals of 1992. Labour MEPs gained the support of the European Parliament for tough environmental standards to be applied to the networks. Recognizing the lack of an overall environmental assessment of the plans, the Parliament proposed a strategic environmental assessment of the impact of a whole network. Previous environmental impact assessments tended only to assess individual 'corridors' and not look at the impact the whole scheme may have on the environment. The proposed guidelines included minimum levels and safeguards for the protection of public health and limitation of environmental nuisance, particularly in terms of sight, noise and vibration. It was also proposed to link the funding of schemes with the new environmental criteria, making it hard for schemes to gain European finance unless they complied with European environmental assessments.

In order to redress the original roads bias in TENS, Labour MEPs proposed a fundamental shift in funding away from roads schemes and towards rail. This related to a minimum 40% funding of railway projects and a maximum 25% funding of road schemes. The Commission is committed to 80% of the funding for the priority projects being directed to the railways. A further 10% will go towards promoting road–rail links and 10% is left to go towards road construction for the first fourteen projects. The point has been made that of the 20,000 km of new road schemes proposed under TENS, most are realignments or upgradings of existing low-quality roads to higher standards. Very little new construction is planned. This funding initiative represents an effort to shift investment from roads to rail in Europe. At present, 80% of all passenger transport in Europe goes by road and just 10% by rail. The Commission has shown a similar commitment to build increased investment in short-sea shipping and canals and rivers into TENS. There are great environmental advantages of sea-going and inland waterway transport that have so far been underutilized.

Accessibility

While Trans-European Networks represent the big idea in European transport policy, it is important that individuals are not ignored in the dash to improve inter-city links and networks. Accessibility to transport for all citizens, from the smallest village to the largest city, must be an essential characteristic of any policy. Europe must show the lead to member states in legislating to make public transport more accessible for those with disabilities. Legislation to provide for the introduction of low-floor buses throughout Europe would be an important first step towards ending exclusion and improving mobility. This is an area where some member states have made greater progress than others. For example, Athens currently has over 600 low-floor buses in operation, compared to a mere 68 operating in London.

One of the keys to regenerating our European cities is to give increased priority to cyclists and pedestrians and accessibility is important here too. Reorganizing urban areas to make them more accessible to cycles and pedestrians and less accessible to motor vehicles can only result in a marked improvement in the quality of life for those who live in the cities of Europe. There are many innovative examples of such urban traffic schemes throughout Europe and these point the way for a European 'reclaiming of cities'. In Copenhagen, an emphasis on cycling accounts for 30% of all home-to-work journeys (compared with 37% for public transport and 30% for private cars). This initiative has resulted in a 10% drop in car traffic in kms per annum compared with 1970. Groningen in The Netherlands goes further. The proportion of cycle traffic amounts to 50% of all trips in the self-styled 'cycle capital of Europe'. By prioritizing the cyclist and pedestrian, streets are made safer, air quality is improved and mobility is increased. At a European level, networks should take account of local urban initiatives and encourage them throughout the European Union. Good practice should be shared and finance made available. The brief for TENS could be widened to include a link between existing national cycle networks and a European cycle network. A similar link could be made to improve access systems for people with disabilities. TENS should be their networks too.

Local Initiatives

Many of these ideas are contained in the concept of a citizen's network, a welcome initiative launched by Neil Kinnock, in a conscious attempt to build passenger priorities into different transport modes in a European framework. Labour believes that Europe can act not just at a transnational or strategic level, but to facilitate local initiatives at the local level. A positive interface between local public transport and TENS needs to be developed.

The European Union is in a position to provide both ideas and resources for local town and city initiatives throughout Europe. It must build upon its successful initiatives such as LIFE and DRIVE. The EU's LIFE programme is a funding initiative that can provide up to 50% of the funds for demonstration projects, awareness campaigns and environmental action. In the UK, the Department of the Environment is reponsible for the initial selection of projects. DRIVE is a research programme which aims to use advanced information technology and communications to improve the performance of passenger and goods transport services. It has funded advanced passenger information services in the UK. The way such funding has been used again demonstrates the link between the environment and transport policy. Two examples of European-funded initiatives in the UK point towards the kind of European transport policy Labour must encourage, that will be more relevant to the citizens of Europe.

Camden Community Transport obtained LIFE finance for an innovative project designed to make community transport more eco-friendly. The project, entitled Accessible Sustainable Transport Integration (ASTI), was launched in April 1995 by Neil Kinnock, who described the scheme as a 'source of stimulation and inspiration towards the fulfilment of series of initiatives to further an effective, integrated and accessible transport system that respects the environment'. The aim of ASTI is to create a network of accessible routes across the southern part of the London Borough of Camden, using gas and electric vehicles and a state-of-the-art computerized scheduling system. The hope is that the scheme will provide a model for accessible, environmentally respectful transport systems throughout Europe.

A similar project, funded by LIFE and designed to address the problems imposed by increasing pressure of motor traffic on a town centre, is in operation in Maidstone, Kent. The Maidstone Initiative for Sustainable Transport (MIST) is a community-wide scheme for Maidstone town centre. The MIST project aims to reduce private commuter car traffic by 15% and increase the public transport share of the travel market by 20%. It aims to reduce carbon dioxide emissions and other pollutants in the area by 20% and provide a self-sufficient local public transport network.

As these sample schemes demonstrate, local empowerment backed by European funding can help to develop accessible and environmentally sustainable transport systems. There are many projects around Europe, such as light rapid transit systems, Manchester metros and innovations like the 'piggyback' scheme to carry freight lorries by rail, that signal the future of transport development. Although many urban initiatives are better dealt with at national and local level, Europe must play a central role in promoting best transport practice, facilitating the exchange of ideas and information, and providing financial assistance where appropriate. The European Union can be a crucial opinion-former in the new transport debate. It can help to re-evaluate the car culture and examine the alternatives. The Commission has pledged to campaign to increase the popularity of underutilised systems such as the railways or short sea shipping.

The New Approach

A comprehensive transport system for Europe in the next millennium must be safe, environmentally sustainable and accessible. The European institutions need to create a network throughout the member states that improves the quality of life for all citizens of Europe while respecting the environment that we, our children and grandchildren will live in. Environmentally sustainable transport will only be achieved if environmental protection and enhancement is put at the core of all transport decisions in Europe. It must not be considered an optional extra.

To bring this about, Labour will undertake to promote a fundamental shift in resources from road to rail, reassess pricing policies to make public transport the most economical option, campaign for the widest possible access to all forms of transport, and will promote urban transport initiatives on a European level. We do not lack the resources. Europe is offering a new approach – recognizing that transport problems must be solved in partnership at the local, national and European level.

The challenge for transport development is an exciting one. Ideas and initiatives are already being developed; it is only the political courage that it is lacking. The Labour Party in Europe has the will and courage to marry these ideas with a positive action plan.[1]

---

[1] I would like to thank Mark Bennister for helping with the research for this chapter.

DAVID THOMAS
From Common Agricultural Policy to Rural Development Policy

The 1996 Intergovernmental Conference (IGC) on the European Union Treaties should provide a backdrop to a fundamental review of the future of the EU. It may also provide a base from which to reconsider the main tenets of those policies which have been pursued for thirty years. One priority for reconsideration must be the policy that receives approximately half the EU budget and yet fails to meet the needs of those it should serve: the Common Agricultural Policy (CAP).

A common agricultural policy was one of the activities of the European Economic Community (as it was then called) listed in Article 3 of the Treaty of Rome. In the treaty chapter entitled 'Agriculture', the common market was extended to agriculture and trade in agricultural products in conjunction with the establishment of a common agricultural policy among member states. Article 39 states that the objectives of the common agricultural policy are:

1 To increase agricultural productivity
2 To ensure a fair standard of living for the agricultural community
3 To stabilize markets
4 To ensure that supplies reach consumers at reasonable prices

In order to achieve these objectives, common organizations of agricultural markets must be established either through (a) common rules on competition; (b) compulsory co-ordination of various national market organizations; or (c) a European market organization. In practice, the third method has been used.

The policy was developed in two stages. The preliminary stage commenced with a conference of member states at which a comparison of their agricultural policies was made and a statement of their resources and needs produced, so that the broad lines of the policy could be formulated. During phase two, the Commission, on the basis of these broad guidelines and having consulted the Economic and Social Committee, submitted proposals to the Council. The six original members of the Community were required to develop and implement the common agriculture policy during a transitional period which terminated at the end of 1969. (Following accession in 1972, the transitional period for introducing the common agricultural policy into Britain terminated in 1977.)

Of all European industries, agriculture is intrinsically linked to the European structure and the ethos of a 'Common Europe'. The Common Agricultural Policy rules, from set-aside to suckler cow premiums, from grubbing-up premiums to agrimonetary arrangements are one of the few policy areas in which spending has shifted either in whole or in part to the Community and national policy is guided by European policy.

Unfortunately, it has also become a monolithic creature, an unwieldy and complicated framework drawn up for a farming world that no longer exists. Almost from its inception, CAP was under pressure to be reformed. Today, radical reform is a matter of urgency and the weight of evidence supporting this view crosses the political spectrum, from Sir Leon Brittan's cabinet reports to 'Secret Garden', the document published in April 1995 by the European Parliament all-party Land Use and Food Policy Inter-group, who are only concerned with budgetary reform. This momentum for change is not just confined to 'European circles': it also has wide-ranging support within the United Kingdom. Documents such as 'European Agricultural Policy – Ten Steps In The Right Direction' (November 1994) by the Royal Institute Of International Affairs, 'Taking Real Choices Forward' by the National Farmers' Union (March 1995), and 'A Rural Policy For Europe' by the Country Landowners Association (April 1995) all support changes of some kind. The Labour Party has entered the debate with its own proposals, 'A Working Countryside' (April 1995), and the British Conservative Government released its own programme in a White Paper on Rural Areas, in October 1995.

While much of the current literature on CAP reform ignores social aspects, the present debate revolves around the recent GATT Agreement and prospects of enlargement to the east, which will have an enormous impact on the Community budget and agricultural prices. As democratic socialists, we must ensure that when change occurs it will benefit the whole rural community and not just a selected few. It is clear in the Communication by Commissioner Fischler to the Madrid Summit on the alternative strategies for agriculture with a view to the accession of the central European countries that the Commission favour a continuation of the measures introduced in 1992. Any change must be carried out in a manner that does not unfairly disadvantage those participating in the present scheme, but the ethos of reform should be to broaden CAP away from a purely 'agriculture' policy to one that encompasses both a food policy with a public health and consumer focus, and a 'rural' policy with a commitment to rural areas generally. Rigid regulation of the agricultural sector has tended to check its adjustment to developments and demands, and indeed the needs and resources of an agricultural policy today are very different from those expressed in post-war Europe in 1958. Changes which have taken place in those policy areas on which agriculture is partly dependent – that is to say, monetary, regional, social and commercial policy – have not coincided with a shift in the foundations of the CAP. This has led to inconsistencies and a lack of policy co-ordination. For example, CAP subsidizes tobacco production whilst the World Health Organization (WHO) is urging people to stop smoking and the Commission is funding anti-smoking campaigns. More serious perhaps is the pursuit of an agri-economic policy which only marginally takes account of contemporary social needs.

Reforming the CAP

Although the task before any CAP reformist may appear daunting, it is not an impossible one. According to 'The Secret Garden', 'the economic means to support reform are available: the question is whether the necessary degree of political will can be created in the run up to the Intergovernmental Conference.'[1] The IGC should construct a long-term practical strategy for reform of the CAP, to provide a more efficient and realistic agriculture/rural/food policy to take Europe into the twenty-first century.

Agricultural policy lies at the heart of the European

[1] 'The Secret Garden', European Parliament Land Use and Food Policy Intergroup, 1995

Union's structure. Although the percentage of the total work-force employed in agriculture in the EU has declined dramatically over the years (21% at the end of the fifties, 7% in the early nineties), agriculture takes up almost half the EU's total budget despite representing only 3.1% of its Gross Domestic Product. In the United Kingdom, the declining number of agricultural workers has been well documented. By 1993 there were only 108,800 full- or part-time workers in England and Wales. As an industry, British agriculture is a minor but significant element of the UK economy. Its contribution to the national GDP has fallen to about 1.3 per cent, and only about 30,000 farm businesses provide employment for ten or more people. At the same time, the industry occupies some 80 per cent of the country's total land area, and provides a home for about a million people including the half a million-strong farm work-force. Rural areas have their own unique problems related to remoteness, transport, employment, and poverty. In the United Kingdom, rural communities have suffered from sixteen years of Conservative 'free market' ideology, the effect of which is illustrated by heavily subsidized farm incomes and prices, combined with the closure of rural schools, shops, post offices and the decline of rural public transport. The uneven distribution of wealth is also striking when one considers that 80% of the CAP funds disbursed go to just 20% of farmers.

In his paper 'A Strategy for British Agriculture: Implications of Future Reforming Pressures' (April 1994), Professor Kenneth J. Thomson notes that the CAP has already been modified since the Treaty of Rome in three fundamental ways. Firstly, in 1969, with the invention of 'green' money and the parallel Monetary Compensatory Amounts (MCAs); followed secondly by the introduction of regional and compensatory subsidies to agriculture in 1975.

Finally, the CAP was modified again in 1984 with the imposition of milk quotas as a new method of supply control, applied effectively at the individual farm level. Europe's first Agriculture Commissioner recognized early on that CAP had a structural tendency to overproduce and overcost. Nevertheless it was only with the reforms of 1992 and the GATT Uruguay Round agreements that the pricing regime was seriously checked. This took the form of a reduction in cereal and beef support prices and the introduction of area and headage compensation payments and semi-compulsory set-aside. These did modify CAP significantly, but did not attempt to redress the treaty provisions which define CAP objectives; nor had the Single European Act or the Maastricht Treaty attempted to redefine the CAP and place it within a modern context. The cornerstones of agricultural policy have remained unmoved for more than thirty years.

Where does Europe go from here? Obviously, change can only take effect if it is backed by a solid political will. No member state or political group should use CAP reform for their own short-term political advantage. To be truly effective, reform must address more significant issues than market mechanisms and pricing policy. In light of the recent enlargement and the likelihood of future expansion, one must begin to question whether the present CAP decision-making structure originally conceived for a Community of six remains suitable for a Union of fifteen or more members. Given the decline in the social and economic fabric of rural communities, it is surely time for the focus of the CAP to shift from that of a 'farming policy' to a coherent policy aimed at sustaining rural economies, producing food which meets criteria other than high production levels, and supporting job creation. Conservation, pollution, animal welfare, recreation, food and poverty are all Europe-wide issues which should be addressed by a modernized rural/agricultural/food policy.

In the Labour Party's document 'A Working Countryside', three broad objectives for future rural policy are set out:

- economic renewal, for the sustainable growth of the rural economy, ensuring a broad range of job opportunities for people in rural areas
- social and democratic renewal, to strengthen and support rural communities
- protection and enhancement of the countryside environment for all who live there, now and in the future.

A radical overhaul of the CAP could bring long-term advantages to rural economies, the environment, consumers and public health. CAP reform could be genuinely popular if it met these broad goals and our energies should be channelled towards that end.

The Legal Basis

If one accepts the overriding view that reform is not only desirable but inevitable if continued confusion and collapse are to be avoided, then the process of decision-making laid down in Articles 38 to 43 of the Treaty of Rome must be the starting point for change. The treaty provisions are the embodiment of the special treatment for which agriculture was singled out, and the source of all agricultural legislation. The Treaty of Rome confers on the Council a general authority to implement the CAP through regulations and directives. The Council exercises this power on the basis of proposals from the Commission. Before taking a decision, the Council must consult the European Parliament, and Parliament must express an opinion. According to the European Court of Justice, failure to do so renders the Council's actions void, but the Council is under no obligation to take account of the Parliament's views. With only fifteen ministers representing some 368.7 million, one wonders to what extent public opinion is being represented in the decision-making process, if at all. Reform must build upon the public debate about Europe's countryside, its products, uses and value. Europe's citizens, after all, pay for the CAP. Their views must be heard. The long-debated 'democratic deficit' is most striking in relation to agriculture, and the role of the European Parliament in the legislative process needs to be addressed urgently.

The basic articles of the Treaty of Rome are clearly out of date and no longer reflect the state of European agriculture as it moves into the next millennium. It is not possible and would serve no purpose to rewrite a chapter of the Treaty of Rome. The point can be illustrated by referring to Articles 38 and 39, which are vivid examples of the outdated philosophy behind the CAP and its increasing failure to reflect a contemporary world view. The definition of an agricultural product in Article 38 as '. . . the products of the soil, of stock-farming and of fisheries . . .' does not take account of the widely held view that animals should be referred to as 'sentient beings'. Indeed, CAP's total failure to consider the animal welfare issue in the definition of CAP illustrates how tentatively the basis of the policy is defined. The objective of the CAP as set out in Article 39, i.e. '. . . to increase agricultural productivity . . .' also belies the fact that European agriculture is far more efficient now than it was forty years ago when the CAP was first being drawn up and Europe was still recovering from the destruction of the Second World War.

That is not to say that nothing of the original ideology should be retained. Indeed, Article 39(b) '... to ensure a fair standard of living for the agricultural community, in particular by increasing the individual earnings of persons engaged in agriculture' should still be part of any future rural strategy in order to maintain or raise the standard of living and quality of life for all those engaged in employment in rural areas. We need to see more people living and working in the countryside. This will be promoted by the inclusion of the accepted threshold for a minimum European rural wage. This threshold, based on the Council of Europe's poverty threshold level of 67% of average national income, should form the basis of an updated Article 39(b). A Europe-wide scheme for the protection of rural workers similar in structure to that of the British Agricultural Wages Board Order 1994, setting out pay and conditions for agricultural workers, should also be incorporated. Finally, although the 1992 reforms introduced certain agri-environmental measures into the CAP, the impact of these measures on the environment is currently marginal. The challenge is to make the whole CAP environmentally friendly.

The Agricultural Budget

European Union budgetary control is crucial if treaty reform is to be effective. EU expenditure is divided into two categories: compulsory (CE) and non-compulsory expenditure (NCE). The European Parliament has little or no say over compulsory expenditure and until recently could not even decide what constitutes or does not constitute CE. Agricultural spending, which accounts for just under 50% of the EU budget, is compulsory. In practice, this means that the European Parliament controls more than 50% of the budget. More effective control of the EU agricultural budget, granting the European Parliament power over the detail of spending rather than forcing it to take an all-or-nothing approach, would allow the elected legislature to act as a proper watch-dog. It would also help to curb the perception of an 'ever-open wallet' that appears to prevail in the public mind.

In order to be effective, our policy review must also tackle the anomalies created by the agrimonetary system and the 'green rate'. The green rate is the special exchange rate used to convert common prices which are fixed annually by the Council of Ministers and expressed in a ratio of ecus to national currencies. The system is designed to protect agricultural prices, incomes and markets from currency fluctuations. This contributes to stabilizing the market since, at a certain level, currency appreciation will result on the one hand in depressed agricultural prices and incomes and, on the other, in increased imports and reduced exports. When a currency depreciates, the reverse is true. This in turn distorts trade in agricultural products and makes prices and incomes unequal. Green rates are regularly readjusted so that they are not divorced from actual exchange rates and when such revaluation takes place, producers receive compensatory payments which are partly funded by the Commission and partly by national budgets. The system was first introduced in 1969 and has been amended on a number of occasions. The present system, introduced in 1992, was intended as a temporary measure which would operate until such a time as a single currency was in place. Not only is it impossible to estimate the cost of the system and thus accurately set the budget, the recent instability in the currency markets has illustrated how expensive the system is to maintain. Indeed, the recent reluctance of those countries with strong currencies to revalue led to a crisis situation whereby, had the system been allowed to continue to operate at the same level, the CAP budget would have been wildly overspent. The Agriculture Council of Ministers agreed a package of reform to the system at their meeting in June 1995, fixing the level of direct aid to farmers at 1995 prices until 1999 and fixing the Commission contribution to compensatory payments at 50%; the remaining 50% being paid by national governments if they wish to do so. Member states may also pay aid to their farmers if they can prove that they have suffered as a result of revaluation in another member state. Although the system has benefited British farmers since the UK's ignoble withdrawal from the ERM in 1992, it was the strong currency countries whose farmers suffered and on whom the burden lay.

Agriculture and the Single Currency

The no-win situation that the agrimonetary system creates results in a high level of political pressure from both European finance ministers and the agricultural community in negotiations. The impact of adjustment to the system on national budgets and farm incomes means that negotiations are hard-fought. Moreover, there is a reluctance to overhaul the system. The economic arguments in favour of the single currency for agriculture are sound – the British National Farmers' Union are themselves advocates of such a scheme, and have stated that 'the agriculture sector would benefit from a single currency'. The view of Mick Sloyan, representing the Meat and Livestock Commission, is that 'The major advantage of such a move is the increased stability and certainty under which the industry would operate.

Farmers would know precisely the value of premium payments and support prices which at present vary the green rate.' Reflected in this view, a single currency is often presented in terms of a threat to sovereignty. The alternative, as is clear from the recent decisions on agrimoney, would have a similar effect to renationalizing agriculture. This is patently absurd. The merits of a single currency are recognized by the business community which longs for the stability this will bring to intra-Community trade, including agriculture.

Employment in Rural Areas

One of the major challenges facing the European Union is how to create employment, particularly in rural areas. If the pressures that the continued rural exodus puts on both abandoned regions and the already overcrowded urban conurbations are to be alleviated, a combined agricultural and environmental policy, encompassed within an effective rural policy, must be developed.

Whilst technological advances have increased agricultural production, they are at the same time responsible for the reduction in agricultural employment. The ability of sustainable agriculture to generate employment requires more extensive study. A report in Britain by the University of Wales on organic farming concluded that employment gains went beyond the farms involved and extended to processing industries. This view appears to have been reinforced by evidence from Germany, where a government-led initiative to reduce surpluses by adopting less intensive farming methods led to the registration of 1500 farmers in one year. A recent study by the environmental organization Friends of the Earth estimated that if one quarter of British farming was converted to organic production, employment in agriculture would increase from 30,000 to 45,000 jobs. The demand for integrated, and less chemically orientated agriculture, horticulture and forestry systems should be considered, not only as an answer to environmental concerns, but also in terms of the capacity for such measures to increase employment. Taking the idea one step further, the feasibility of any new rural-policy funding scheme to encourage farmers to adapt their farming methods to make farming more environmentally friendly should be studied. Such a funding scheme could be based on an assessment scale. The more environmentally effective the activities of a farmer/landowner, the more funding he would receive. A similar scheme could be used to encourage a conversion programme to organic production with a view to emphasizing environmental awareness, job creation and consumer/public demands and a less intensive system of farming. But this in itself will not lead to full employment in agriculture. For a variety of reasons (specific abilities which are not transferred easily, concentration of training schemes in urban areas, remoteness, lack of job opportunities, etc.), those employed in agriculture have a particularly low occupational mobility, while investment is often concentrated in and around urban areas. A comprehensive rural policy must look realistically at alternative job creation, in areas such as tourism, reforestation, craft industries and community services.

One group facing particularly severe problems in rural communities is women, whose disadvantages merit specific attention. It is hard to determine the number of women working in the rural economy, for many contribute significantly without independent recognition of their status, as the distinction between domestic and professional responsibilities is often blurred. Nevertheless, it is estimated that women represent nearly 35% of the agricultural workforce. The economic crisis, combined with the long-term increased demand by women for recognition and social rights, has prompted more women to search for employment to supplement household budgets.

Until now, programmes aimed at enhancing the position of women in rural economies have been rather experimental and *ad hoc*. Potential employment in small manufacturing businesses, agricultural food product enterprises, craft industries, services and tourism has remained largely under-exploited, as has teleworking, which can provide possibilities for women in remoter areas or those seeking to combine family responsibilities with gainful employment.

The necessary incentives for small and medium-sized enterprises to invest in rural areas must be coupled with appropriate vocational training so that women may take full advantage of the increased opportunities. However, such measures will only be successful if the infrastructure and services are such as to allow their participation. Child care, transport and replacement services are an essential part of rural policy. Connected with this is the burden of a rising ageing population on women in rural areas, as it tends to be women who provide care for elderly relatives. Remoteness tends to deny them adequate information and support. Formal recognition and remuneration for the service they provide would benefit women and elderly alike. The increased provision of care and leisure facilities required to cope with the shift in the demographic makeup of the rural community is a key area in which the burden on women should be alleviated, and another source of potential employment at which training should be targeted. This could give real meaning to the current character of much of the UK Conservative Government's 'care in the community' programme – a misnomer if ever there was one.

Animal Transportation

With employment and consumer demands in mind, an in depth study should be made into greater control of animal transportation, through restricted journey times and the ancillary effect this would have on employment if more meat were carried on the 'hook' and not the 'hoof'.

In the United Kingdom, the issue of animal transportation is emotive and needs to be examined in a logical and practical way. It should be incorporated into any future European rural policy, as animal transportation and welfare and its implications for consumers is very much a matter of concern to the general public. If minimizing long-distance travel is the solution, then the mechanisms for delivering policy can best be addressed at European level. The subject is pressing. The flow of live animals across borders is rapidly increasing. This is clearly illustrated if we examine the number of live sheep transported out of the United Kingdom since 1986. In 1986 it was recorded at 187,000 live sheep, rising to almost 1.5 million in 1992 – an increase of 700% in just six years from the United Kingdom alone. Any European rules governing animal transportation must take into account the varying attitudes of member states towards animal welfare. However, differing interpretations of rules and regulations often cause complication and conflict, and such European regulation must be drawn up clearly and concisely, leaving little scope for misinterpretation. This issue has been dealt with on several occasions by the European Parliament and, as recently as February 1995, the Parliament passed a resolution calling on the

Council to 'take an immediate decision on uniform rules for the transport of animals in the EU' and for it to 'provide for animal transportation journeys to be limited to a maximum of eight hours, and to lay down clear standards for land, sea and air journeys, with regular monitoring by veterinary bodies so that transport conditions improve'. The principle that slaughter should be carried out as near to the point of production as possible should underlie the eventual policy. It is contended that in this way rural communities could benefit from an increase in employment and greater support for the local economy. It is clear that, once set, the standards must be overseen with proper and effective powers of enforcement in order to ensure fair play and prevent abuse of the system on the basis that 'everyone else ignores the rules', as is sadly often the case in many community policy areas.

The Agriculture Council of Ministers meeting in June 1995 agreed certain measures on the transportation of live animals. These were based around an overall journey time of eight hours with a variation depending on the type of vehicle used or animal being transported. Although this agreement is not perfect, it is a start and continued effort should be made to reach an agreement that is both workable and acceptable to people interested in the issue of live animal transportation and its surrounding problems.

Conclusion

It is of course relatively easy to reform the CAP with admirable sentiments whilst ignoring practical considerations. Realization of such policy objectives would involve substantial financial investment. Given the present economic climate in all member states, there is a reluctance to increase Community contributions significantly. But does reform of the CAP necessarily require that additional funds be made available? At the moment, rural communities benefit from a number of funding programmes, many of which potentially overlap or have similar criteria. With so many funding schemes, there is a potential risk of waste or of a few being eligible for several grants while others receive nothing. It is suggested that any reform of the CAP should include in its remit an analysis of the various schemes and their cost-effectiveness. Individual funding schemes provide for only a small part of ERDF funding, approximately 9%, and allow funds to be focused on industries facing particular difficulties. Any review should be carried out with a remit not to change or cancel these schemes, but to improve their acccessibility and to guard against overlap.

Reform is never an easy path. The increasing realization and acceptance that reform must go beyond attempts to fine-tune a machine which is past its best presents a unique opportunity to establish the legal basis for policies which will reopen village shops, pubs and post offices, which will get trains and buses running again, and which will provide homes to meet real social needs rather than developers' greed. The starting point of CAP reform should not be to enlarge the budget but rather to streamline and retarget existing funds to meet the needs of the rural economy as a whole. Regeneration of Europe's rural communities can only be realistically achieved if sectoral reform is linked to the removal of the restrictive scope of Articles 39 to 43 of the European treaties, so that associated policies and instruments become an integral part of a policy which will ensure survival and prosperity for rural communities in Europe into the twenty-first century.

ANITA POLLACK
Europe and the Environment

What Crisis?

We are living beyond the limits of the earth's capacity. It is this knowledge, and the need to do something about it, which motivates environmentalists.

Despite the slogan, 'think global, act local', Europe is one of the most important arenas in which we can promote a shift in favour of the environment. Action at the European level has an effect at all levels: not only nationally, regionally and locally, but also at the level of international conventions and treaties.

Today's acknowledged environmental crises make a long list: global warming; air, water, noise and toxic waste pollution; holes in the ozone layer; acid rain; deforestation; desertification; overpopulation; dangerous nuclear installations and unprotected nuclear waste; overfishing . . . and so on.

There will be no attempt here to analyse all these problems. However, a look at just a few examples shows us how crucial it is that action and forward planning are taken in the next few years.

Global Warming

There are still a few diehards around who refuse to acknowledge that the climate is changing. Other people simply think that global warming means they will be able to sit in their gardens for summer barbecues without worrying about the weather. The reality is rather different.

As a result of global warming, the polar ice-caps are melting faster than usual, causing rising sea levels which threaten a large number of coastal cities (and which may eventually drown parts of Bangladesh, The Netherlands, the Maldives and many smaller Pacific Islands), and putting millions of lives at risk. Shifts in climate will increasingly bring droughts, floods, famines and pests, with horrendous effects on the natural world and the rate at which species become extinct.

The growing unpredictability of our weather patterns has already had an effect on the insurance industry. In 1992 total financial losses from weather-related disasters cost $23 billion. These losses lead to higher and higher premiums, which will rebound on both industry and individuals.

Carbon emissions

World carbon emissions from fossil fuel burning have climbed steadily, more than tripling over the past half-century. CO_2 emissions in the EU are at twice the world average. As a response to this, several leading nations signed up to the Framework Convention on Climate Change at the Earth Summit in Rio de Janeiro in June 1992, since ratified by over a hundred countries. The Rio signaturies pledged to stabilize CO_2 emissions at 1990 levels by the year 2000 – a goal felt to be inadequate by most environmentalists. Yet even this target now looks unlikely to be achieved. To compound the problem, there has been a hostile response from developing countries (particularly in Asia and Latin America), who are expected to double their output of CO_2 in the next fourteen years.

Clean green energy

According to scientific reports from the American environmental organisation Worldwatch, carbon emissions will have to be reduced by between 60 and 80% if further global warming is to be prevented. But they are currently projected to *increase* by 60% over the next two decades.

The Tories have been congratulating themselves on meeting their Rio targets for the UK (by decimating the coal-mining industry, switching to gas and continuing to subsidize nuclear energy). But energy saving measures, both in Britain and Europe, are totally inadequate, and the jobs which could be created as a result of a decent energy policy aren't there. Privatised energy utilities seek to maximise shareholders' profits by selling more gas and electricity and have no interest in energy saving.

Many in Europe and the USA are arguing for some kind of energy (or CO_2) tax. This has been a sticking point for the Labour Party because of the row in the UK over VAT on fuel, and because of fears that a rise in energy prices may hit the poor. Any kind of energy tax would have to be designed to target high-energy users and not penalize low-income groups.

A British Labour Government will have to introduce some kind of eco-tax reform: the problems simply will not be solved by other means. To do so, Labour will have to face up to restructuring the tax system so as to reward energy-saving, recycling and the use of renewable resources, and penalize fossil-fuel burning, pollution and the unsustainable use of resources.

Combined heat and power (co-generation) is the cheapest form of thermal power generation and gives substantial emission reduction benefit. It saves the heat wasted in the power generation process, so that it can be used for industry, commerce and home heating. According to a study published by COGEN, combined heat and power could be supplying 30% of European electricity needs.[1] This figure has already been achieved in Finland, but in the rest of the EU it is a paltry 6%. The political will to make the changes has so far been missing. Labour's agenda in Europe must prioritize energy saving.

Nuclear Energy

A group of MEPs in the European Parliament are currently concerned with finding means to help clean up and close down dangerous nuclear installations in Central and Eastern Europe and the CIS. The precarious state of many of these installations could conceivably lead to accidents so terrible that they would make the Chernobyl disaster look mild.

Nuclear waste is another concern: for example, a Norwegian environmental group has uncovered evidence in the Arctic area of Russia of wholesale dumping of nuclear waste and abandoned nuclear submarines; and more evidence is coming to light about the massive contamination of vast tracts of land and water in Russia.

Nuclear energy is a sticky issue for a Labour Government. But as things now stand, with no one knowing what to do about nuclear waste, it is high time Labour took a stronger line against nuclear energy.

[1] *The Barriers to Combined Heat and Power*, COGEN Europe, 1995.

Crisis on the Eastern Front

There are appalling environmental conditions on our doorsteps as a consequence of the poisoned air, soil and water of large parts of Central and Eastern Europe and the CIS. To some extent, the European Union is already helping to foot the bill for the clean-up (some estimates of the total cost are as high as $300 billion). But the immensity of that task must be acknowledged and quantified in any debates about enlargement. There are clear political arguments for embracing the former communist bloc, but the huge environmental costs of enlarging the EU have not been discussed openly enough within the UK Labour movement.

In Bulgaria, three-quarters of the water is polluted and almost half the arable land either eroded or polluted by toxic chemicals. In Poland, 95% of surface water has been declared unfit for human consumption. In the Czech Republic, 60% of forests are damaged by air pollution, and half the drinking water is industrially polluted. In 1990, Czech government statistics estimated that pollution had reduced the country's GNP by 7% and life expectancy by seven years below that of Western Europeans. In an area known as the Black Triangle (Upper Silesia, North Bohemia and Saxony), the worst pollution in Europe contributes 30% of Europe's sulphur dioxide and 20% of its nitrogen dioxide emissions.

Cars and Healthy Cities

The problems of pollution are most noticeable in urban areas, where 90% of British people live. Here, the quality of life is being hit in dozens of ways, many of them due to traffic. Private mobility on demand was seen until recently as a basic freedom. But noise, vibration, dirt and traffic fumes now cause respiratory illnesses, provoke stress and ruin town centres. Congestion and poor quality of life also threaten jobs: new industries and businesses do not want to move to environmentally degraded areas.

The Royal Commission's report on *Transport and the Environment*[2] concluded that the government's transport policy was characterized by 'a disregard for the environmental consequences of growth in motor traffic, a preoccupation with road building at the expense of other modes and a failure to appreciate the links between land use planning and transport'. The Conservative's obsession with what Margaret Thatcher dubbed 'the great car economy' has also had profound effects on people's health. The nasty cocktail of pollutants released from motor exhausts has led to a marked increase in respiratory problems: prescriptions for asthma treatments doubled in the UK between 1982 and 1991. Yet the UK Department of Transport estimates that road traffic is likely to increase by anything up to 142% by the year 2025.

A Labour Government must tackle these issues on a number of fronts, including re-creating a reliable, safe and affordable public transport system, and making it possible for there to be a modal shift of freight off the roads and on to the railways.

The European Commission is funding an expert group on 'the car of the future' (mainly composed of industrialists and academics, not environmentalists) to look at ideas for future legislation. Despite the existence of a massive car industry lobby, the European Parliament is constantly pushing for ever-tighter standards for vehicle emissions, and

---

[2] *Transport and the Environment*, Royal Commission on Environmental Pollution, HMSO, 1994.

Labour can play a strong role in supporting these initiatives.

Many tough decisions ranging from vehicle emissions to local traffic planning will have to be taken during the next decade and much of the detail will pass through the European Parliament. It will need positive support from a Labour Government at European, national and local levels to reach workable solutions.

Greeny-red Economics

There used to be an antagonism between the environmental movement and the business community. Industrialists believed that environmental protection and economic growth were mutually exclusive, whilst certain environmentalists were against the idea of growth altogether. The Vice-President of the USA, Al Gore, has described this era as one of 'false choices and short-sighted policies'.[3] Since the late 1980s, there has been a growing realization that the goals of a prosperous economy and a clean environment are not mutually exclusive, that economic growth demands environmental protection, and that jobs can actually be created through protecting the environment.

The Bruntland Report[4] has done much to promote the concept of sustainable development – learning to live within our ecological means. For far too long, people have treated natural resources as mere commodities, to be sacrificed on the altar of economic growth. Living within our ecological means involves 'taking nature into account' in calculating

---

[3] *Earth in the Balance*, Al Gore, Earthscan, 1992.
[4] *Our Common Future*, World Commission on Environment and Development, OUP, 1987.

growth, GNP and the price of goods, taxing environmental 'evils' (such as pollution) rather than economic 'goods' (such as labour), and providing fiscal incentives and disincentives to encourage ecologically sound behaviour.

As customers demand cleaner products and as legislation ensures that these are in turn produced more cleanly, any businesses which refuse to evolve are likely to lose out. Conversely, those businesses which use up fewer resources, conserve more energy and recycle more waste will find their markets expanding.

The OECD has estimated that the world-wide market for environmental goods and services in 1990 was some $200 billion and that 1.7 million people in the EU are already directly employed in the environment industry, and this number is expected to continue to rise. This is about the size of the European chemical industry. A further growth of 50% is forecast by the year 2000. Those countries with the strictest environmental legislation – such as Germany, Sweden and Denmark – have already cornered the largest share of the growing environmental technology market. German industry has now voluntarily agreed to reduce CO_2 emissions or specific energy consumption by 20% by the year 2005.

During the years of Tory government, the UK's once booming environmental industry has suffered from a lack of investment and a de-regulated climate. As EU legislation on the environment becomes stricter, and as cleaner, greener industries replace their polluting forebears, it becomes less likely that environmentally conscious companies will want to invest in Britain. This is bad news for British industry and British jobs.

Investment in long-term environmental programmes also generates employment. In the US, for example, 80,000 jobs have been created as a result of investment in energy efficiency within the electricity industry. The Association for the Conservation of Energy estimates that a similar programme in Britain could create up to 50,000 permanent jobs. Labour has consistently advocated such a programme, but has been stonewalled by a government which refuses to accept that there are times when government intervention is needed to overcome market failures.

'The question is not one of choosing between jobs and environmental protection,' a recent European Commission paper concluded. 'The only viable and lasting solution may be a strategy that addresses both concerns at the same time.'[5] Despite opposition from some trade unions, Labour seems to be coming round to the same conclusion.

Green Accounting

If we do not take urgent action for our environment, the whole web of human economic activity is threatened. 'Ecology' and 'economy' come from the same root – the word 'eco', meaning house. The link is clear. We must take into account what the cost (not simply in financial terms) will be if environmental protection is *not* implemented.

The search for a valid system of green accounting is now taking place, from Europe to India, from Costa Rica to Sweden. Traditional macroeconomic indicators, such as GNP and national income (calculated under the United Nations System of National Accounts), do not accurately reflect the effects of economic activities on nature. This failure helps to perpetuate the present over-consumption of

---

[5] *Economic Growth, Employment and Environmental Sustainability*, European Commission, 1993.

resources and thus increases pollution. Estimates have shown that we are currently losing, on average, around 10% of GNP in both 'developed' and 'developing' countries.

A shift to green accounting requires a partnership between economists, Treasury ministers, industry, academics and environmentalists. In particular, the EU should start publishing ecological and social indicators on a regular basis to accompany the publication of macroeconomic indicators such as GNP. A forward-thinking Labour Government should be part of a European effort to develop more accurate indicators of economic progress.

People Power

Recent protests about road building, animal transport and the Criminal Justice Act have shown a real demand by citizens to have their points of view taken into consideration. People are prepared to take public action in defence of their environment, whether by demonstrations or civil disobedience, to make their views felt.

There are lessons here for a Labour Government. If environmental policy does not win public support, it will not succeed. A commitment to people power must be more than simply rhetorical. Public access to environmental information is an essential factor here. Access to information is a fundamental right of all citizens, and it can best be guaranteed through legally binding measures. A voluntary approach, or one based solely on the selective provision of information by public authorities, is inadequate. In particular, people must have the right to be heard and the right to appeal. The EU should strengthen its legislation on access to environmental information so as to ensure these rights.

In Europe, the EU Directive on Freedom of Access to Environmental Information[6] is perhaps the most significant piece of legislation as far as freedom of information is concerned, as it is legally binding on EU member states. However, although it has led to some improvements in environmental transparency, it still contains weaknesses and some member states have failed to enforce its provisions.

The main thrust of an access-to-information policy ought to be that everyone has a right of access to environmental information, without having to prove an interest. Public participation should be encouraged by such provisions as notice requirements, public distribution of draft legislation proposals at an early stage, and the publication of reasoned decisions. Whenever possible this should be complemented by the publication of easily understood but objective information about policies and projects.

The concept of shared responsibility, with all sections of society acting in partnership, is crucial. Lack of basic environmental information has frequently undermined the efforts of individuals, community groups, environmental organizations and even elected representatives, effectively to confront environmentally destructive practices. One idea being put forward is to create a fund which NGOs could use in protests against environmentally unsound projects.

Red or Green, or Red and Green?

British mainstream political parties seem to feel that the environmental crisis is of little interest to voters. Yet much

[6] Com (90/313/EEC).

of the grassroots political activity of recent years has been broadly 'green' in character.

On the Continent, and especially in Scandinavia, Germany and The Netherlands, environmental concerns are at the forefront of political thinking. In Britain, the left has traditionally tended to concentrate on issues such as jobs, housing, health and education and allowed the environment to be sidelined. Yet the environment impacts on all these other areas, and the pivotal influence it has on our quality of life should place it at the heart of socialism.

Many socialists traditionally believed that environment policy would hinder economic growth and lead to unemployment, but these ideas are outdated. It is now clear that a progressive environmental policy can lead to improved economic performance and jobs, and that a range of sensibly directed policy actions can contribute to social justice. This thesis is developed in the Friends of the Earth pamphlet on jobs and the environment.

Labour's policy document on the environment, *In Trust for Tomorrow*, agreed at the Labour Party Annual Conference in 1994, sets out the guidelines for Labour's environment policy in government, which will also need to be pursued in Europe. Its four key themes are:

- the need to place the environment at the heart of all areas of policy
- that effective environmental protection requires the whole range of government action and cannot rely on the free market
- that high environmental standards drive economic efficiency
- that environmental progress and social equity go hand in hand

The free market alone cannot save anyone's environment.

A firm combination of legislation and new initiatives, backed by a Labour Government playing an active role in European and international policy agreements, is the only way to make progress. Britain, acting hand in hand with its European partners, can help Europe to lead the way in setting targets at an international level and bringing about a real change at home.

The long, hard years of Tory rule in Britain have established our reputation as 'the dirty man of Europe'. Not only has the government delayed and weakened European environmental legislation, it has also irritated our neighbours by refusing to tackle toxic waste and sewage pollution of the North Sea, and nuclear contamination of the Irish Sea.

The vast majority of environmental issues cannot be tackled at a national level. This is why the European Parliament has so much influence in this area. The arrival of lead-free petrol, clean drinking water and catalytic converters (amongst other advances), were all accelerated by Labour and Socialist Members of the Environment Committee.

Labour's European Agenda

The most important way in which a Labour Government can help push forward sustainable development in Europe is through its actions in the Council of Ministers simply by supporting rather than blocking and delaying environmental legislation.

Here are some items for a progressive Labour European Agenda:

- Fight environmental roll-back. There are strong

pressures to deregulate and cut back on environmental legislation.[7] Labour must oppose this and instead improve standards.
- Support the development of green accounting.
- Tackle car dependency and promote a sustainable transport strategy for Europe. This means prioritizing rail rather than road links in the Trans-European Networks for a start.
- Insist on high standards in water and air quality.
- Favour reducing labour costs through increased pollution charges – as advocated in the Delors White Paper.[8]
- Push for watchdog status for the European Environment Agency when its remit is reviewed in 1997.
- Demand tough environmental clean-up conditions for the entry of Central and Eastern European countries into the EU. This may mean paying a price in higher financial contributions to the EU.
- Resist the free-market, voluntarist approach to environmental protection. Labour must insist that the free market cannot solve all environmental problems, and that legislation is necessary.
- Support and promote greater energy saving, combined heat and power and the use of renewables.
- Demand strict environmental criteria for all projects funded by the EU, including Regional and Cohesion Funds, PHARE and TACIS and other financial instruments.
- Press for an international labelling system on tropical hardwood and help promote sustainably managed

---

[7] For example, the Molitor Report on Legislative and Administrative Simplification, European Commission, 1995.
[8] White Paper on Growth, Competitiveness and Employment, European Commission, 1993

forests, with a ban on European imports of timber from non-compliant sources.
- Push for more open EU decision-making, including simplified and real access to environmental information and wider environmental impact assessment. There should be a full and public appraisal of all policy proposals.

People are looking for a better quality of life. They want to be able to walk in the woods without seeing trees dying of acid rain, to bathe in clean waters and breathe clean air. They do not want to hand on a dying world to their children.

Much more could be done. A progressive Labour Government could help Europe lead the way in saving the world's environment. The pollution of large numbers of the world's rivers and lakes, pillaging of the world's tropical forests and degradation of the lives of millions of the world's people are increasing at an alarming rate. We have come close to killing the earth. The Labour Party, if it seeks to govern Britain in the near future, must put environmental issues at the centre of its activities. In doing so, it will inevitably place us at the heart of Europe.[9]

---

[9] I would like to thank Gareth Harding for his contribution.

PHILLIP WHITEHEAD
Protecting the Citizen as Consumer

Consumers were barely mentioned in the original Treaty of Rome. Even now, Community law defines a consumer as 'a person who concludes a contract for a purpose which can be regarded as being outside his or her trade or profession'. Thirty-five years ago, when we still lay offshore from the new Europe, Michael Young warned in *The Chipped White Cups of Dover* that citizens' outrage at faulty or shabby goods would become potent: 'politics will become less and less the politics of production and more and more the politics of consumption'.[1] The left declined to publish the pamphlet; the dignity of labour was affronted by this attack on its producer role.

The word consumer still produces mixed vibrations. Consumers can be seen narrowly as maximizing personal satisfaction through the judicious use of their spending power. But they can also evaluate goods and services in a social as well as a personal context. The good consumer knows that protection through knowledge, testing, and equal standards helps all citizens, that best-buy transport is not the motorway toll road and that a hospital operation

[1] Michael Young, *The Chipped White Cups of Dover*, October 1960, p. 11.

should not be preceded by a wallet biopsy.

In so far as the Treaty of Rome effected an improvement in 'social cohesion and solidarity among member states',[2] it was largely through the impetus and initiative deployed by the great producer interests. *They* made a market. Consumers have been forced to be reactive; although in some of the member states (The Netherlands, Belgium and the UK particularly), powerful, independent consumer organizations are now entrenched. But as the expanding Community moved to the Single European Act it offered a challenge to cartels and price-fixing because they obstructed 'market liberalization'. Consumer protection directives carry the mantra that they are 'essential to achieving free movement of goods and hence completing the internal market'.

We should remember that even the limited achievements of European consumer protection have little relevance to much of the world beyond the EU. Citizen's initiatives in the Third World are direct, brave and basic. Getting the information into the small print of the label or the contract only helps if you can read and understand the small print, and make effective substitution choices. That is not the position of the nursing mother at the mercy of unscrupulous multinational pushers of breast-milk substitutes in Bangladesh, or the gullible watcher of TV-advertising in Belarus for tobacco products which are banned in the West.

Consumer campaigners in the developing world risk life itself in their advocacy, and the better-informed consumers of the European Community should never forget the world beyond the single market, which takes so many of its products, with so little of its capacity for information and redress.

---

[2] Treaty Establishing the European Community (signed in Rome on 25 March 1957), Article 2.

In 1975, the EC's Council of Ministers adopted the first Consumer Information and Protection Programme, which outlined five basic consumer rights:

- Economic Justice
- Access to Redress
- Protection of Health and Safety
- Information and Education
- Representation and Participation

At the same time, the Commission set up its own Consumers' Consultative Committee (CCC) to work with an independent service for 'the protection of the consumer and the environment'. The European Parliament established a committee of oversight, the Environment, Public Health and Consumer Protection Committee, the following year, which has developed over the past two decades into one of the largest, most active and interventionist of all of the committees.

The large majority of consumer protection measures brought forward between 1979 and 1994 were justified by their importance in facilitating the common, and later the single market. A series of directives on the labelling, presentation and advertising of foodstuffs began in 1978. The labelling and advertising of medicinal products followed. Measures intended to set Community-wide standards for package holidays, product safety, unfair terms in consumer contracts, non-life, vehicle and life insurance, and consumer credit have been introduced but not always implemented, and they are still a long way from that comprehensive protection of the consumer as a citizen of the European Community which all who seek a positive role for regulation within the single market would desire. Standards do not conform to best practice within the member states. Choice, information and redress are frustrated by national boundaries and restrictive practices, and the consumer interest is not taken into account in other key policy areas like agriculture, transport and communications. Nor are there the necessary competencies in the Maastricht Treaty to make them so.

Before Maastricht, the emphasis had remained on the effectiveness of the internal market. In 1992 the report of the Sutherland Group[3] was published on the initiative of two forceful advocates of strength through competitiveness, Commissioners Van Miert and Bangemann. This report seemed complacent about the reality of such a market for consumers, especially those whose limited economic means and access to information gave them the greatest proportionate need. A much tougher approach championing the consumer cause was required. In this context, as in others, Maastricht flattered to deceive. Article 129a of the new Treaty provided a baseline for a European consumer policy, stating that:

> The Community shall contribute to the attainment of a high level of consumer protection through:
> a Measures adopted pursuant to Article 100a in the context of the completion of the internal market;
> b Specific action which supports and supplements the policy pursued by the member states to protect the health, safety and economic interests of consumers, and to provide adequate information to consumers.

The co-decision procedures, involving the European Parliament in a joint resolution of areas of difference which emerge with the Council and the Commission, is applied to all legislation falling under Article 129a. This has led to some improvements, such as the 1994 Directive on time-

---

[3] Named after its Chairman, former European Competition Commissioner Peter Sutherland.

share purchases, which after co-decision discussions provided for a brief cooling-off period for intending purchasers to reflect on the specified written contract, and to withdraw and cancel the arrangement if they saw fit. Like the various package holiday directives, however, it leaves many loopholes because the Community cannot, as yet, provide international legal standards to cover cross-border disputes about property law.

The existence of Article 129a has been of limited use to date as a legal basis for consumer action. Only one directive, introducing a Community system of information on home and leisure accidents, has been based on it.

After twenty years, how near to achievement are the five basic rights paraded by the Council in 1975? There is now a congealed mass of legislation in place, intended to protect the health and safety of consumers, and to assert their economic interest *vis-à-vis* producers. But there is no framework of measures which gives consumers greater legal protection. They do not have a formal role in the procedures of consultation, and information about what rights do and do not exist is limited. The five basic consumer rights remain basic, but they have not yet been given the status of rights.

Economic justice

Economic justice involves allowing consumer interests into the full range of legislation which impinges on them, be it financial, technical or agricultural. Only through this will the consumer get the level of protection in the market place to which he or she is entitled. It has to be said that the record is blemished. Voluntary provisions, weak enforcement and inadequate monitoring have dogged directives down the years. Without minimum standards of enforcement, mutually supported by the member states, there will be no proper pursuit of justice.

Tawney famously remarked of the unregulated market that freedom for the pike means death for the minnows. In the single market, the pike argue that they are very small pike by world standards and that their useful work of keeping the waters of the pool turbulent will be damaged if they have to adjust to the needs of its other denizens. The minnows are told that they are necessary for the food chain, that the pond could not go on without them, but the pike must be left to their own devices, if only they will voluntarily curb their appetites.

Financial services

The mixture of exhortation and lacklustre pursuit is well illustrated in the field of financial transactions, which ought to be at the cutting edge of the single market. Cross-border payments, the regulation of credit used therein, and distance-selling generally have not benefited from a rigorous approach. Every citizen who has changed money at a frontier, or made a purchase in a different currency, is fully aware of the problem.

In the matter of cross-border payments it took more than three years for a Payment Systems Users' Liaison Group set up by the Commission to stumble towards the basis for a directive, despite the evidence that SMEs were gravely handicapped by delays and surcharges. A series of surveys[4] showed that cross-border payments were often delayed, that the proportion of low-value transactions absorbed by charges was high, and that there were problems with double-charging, lack of transparency and compensation for 'lost' payments.

Throughout this time, pious Recommendations (1990)

[4] J. Mitchell, *Banking World*, March 1995, p. 27.

and Communications (1993) from the Commission gave the banks an extended remit for voluntary action. In practice, by 1994 only 14% of banking branches visited in the EU by an independent research organization could provide written information for customers on the options, time and cost of the services they offered.[5] Now, years too late, a draft directive has been introduced to outlaw double-charging, compensation if the permitted maximum working days for transactions are exceeded, and full information about their terms, conditions and timetable.

The wider field of consumer credit remains to be tackled. With the explosion in communications, when satellite TV and the Internet message cross all frontiers more easily than we now ride beneath the Channel, cross-border shopping will soar above its current 3% of transactions within the single market. With this will come the international version of the loan-shark, taking advantage of consumers who make a decision far from home, or with inadequate information about the long-term commitments they are making. Invariably such people are vulnerable and most in need of the protection which an unregulated market would never give them. A German consumer consultant sums up the fallacy of the anti-regulators: 'The starting-point for EU policy neglects the fact that many consumer problems cannot be solved through market competition, e.g. the social consequences of over-indebtedness. The private household is not comparable to the economic mechanisms of a business.'[6]

The Consumer Credit directive of 1987 placed only the

[5] Ibid, p. 28.
[6] Rainer Metz, North Rhein Westphalia Consumer Centre, quoted in J. Lowe, 'Regulating cross-border credit', *Consumer Policy Review*, Volume 5, No. 2, April 1995, p. 55.

feeblest restraint on the abuse of credit practices, requiring the APR to be printed in advertisements and contracts, and bringing in conditions governing repossession of goods and early repayment. These applied to transactions up to 2000 ecu, and excluded loans to buy property, hire agreements and charge cards. The directive also averted its eyes from the troubled question of how the credit market should be policed. It thus offered few external protections of the kind routinely applied in the UK since the Consumer Credit Act of 1974, much less improve on them. Even in Britain, dodgy credit-sharks are not unknown, despite the Office of Fair Trading's database of banned individuals – one in two hundred of those licensed to practise. As cross-border financial transactions, including loans, increase, a database of credit providers throughout the Community will be urgently required. Without a system of licensing throughout the Community, and an acknowledgement of lender liability in cross-border transactions involving the purchase of goods by credit card, Europe can hardly be said to be pursuing economic justice for those who need it most.

The saga of the current Distance Selling draft directive illustrates the problem of securing robust Community action. The potential benefits of distance selling, if the rules are not tilted against the buyer, are considerable. It allows the buyer to be a participant in a far wider market, able to shop around much more. However, the expansion of cross-border selling by telephone, TV videotext and fax referred to above has also produced many concerns. The Commission proposes to regulate the soliciting of orders, effective delivery of goods or services, and a right of withdrawal from certain contracts.

The UK government, however, with tacit support from two other member states, proposed in the Council of Ministers the exclusion of banking, consumer credit, and all investment and insurance services, on the grounds that these were already covered by specific EC and national regulations, irrespective of whether they were 'negotiated at a distance'. None of the latter went as far as the draft directive, although it has become clear that it is the financial sector that is set to make the most use of the new techniques.

The consumer also faces producers and service providers who ignore the aspirations of the single market when it suits them. Banks, manufacturers and major retail outlets all attempt to preserve their own home markets and high price differentials. You cannot buy the same car at the same price throughout the Community and the differences often have little to do with the distance of the vendor from the country of manufacture. For example, a Ford Scorpio can be bought 55.5% more cheaply in Italy than in neighbouring Austria.[7] Car-makers, including those of the UK, have been able to prolong for a further seven years the arrangement whereby dealers are tied to a single manufacturer. Proper on-site comparisons are hard to come by.

Consumer contracts

European Institutions frequently fail to take action to protect the consumer against infringements of the treaties. The directive on Unfair Terms in Consumer Contracts, first proposed by the Commission in 1990, covers all contracts made by a consumer with persons acting in the course of their trade, business or profession. Much of this is vitiated, however, by the long list of exclusions in contracts concluded away from business premises, and by the lack of effective penalties. Because of the permissive nature of the

---

[7] Car prices within the European Union on 1 May 1995: survey carried out by Directorate General IV (Competition) of the Commission of the European Communities.

directive, it has been possible for the British government to confer legal standing only on its own agent, the Director General of Fair Trading, as competent to bring class actions under the 1994 Regulation which incorporates the EC directive into British law.

Citizens and legitimate consumer groups will sometimes be better judges of whether such actions should be brought, and the Consumers' Association (CA) has gone to court to apply for a judicial review of the Government's interpretation of the directive. If the Consumers' Association action succeeds in the British and European courts, there will be a far broader basis for the entrenchment of good practice through the actions of consumers themselves.

Advertising

Another example of the consumer being too easily duped is the case of unfair or misleading advertising. Directives on Comparative and Misleading Advertising have addressed the issues of subliminal methods and unfair stereotyping. They have not managed to define unfairness towards individuals or groups, nor to provide means of redress for those who may have been misled by advertisements into purchasing goods or a service. This is particularly the case with the ineffective regulation of distance selling described above, and the blandishments of the package travel trade.

Tourism

Tourism is not yet an area of specific competence for the European Union, so there is no direct legal basis for European action to protect those who use the products and services of this new boom industry. The uses of leisure is an area of substantial conflict in the EU.

Tourists have a serious need for prompt access to justice, and to an internationally reorganized complaints procedure.

The Green Paper on Tourism produced by Commissioner Papoutsis needs to take as its purpose the overall protection of tourists, their safety and well-being. Whether the problem is overbooking, sudden price surcharges, lack of provision for disabled people or the existence of fire and poisoning hazards, Europe's citizens need protection.

Agriculture

It has been proposed that over time the Common Agricultural Policy will be shifted away from a system whereby producers are rewarded by intervention payments for overproducing at the consumer's expense to one where their support on the margin comes from payments for the stewardship of the land itself. Amenity would have a higher priority in any scheme which valued extensive husbandry as seriously as the CAP now values intensive farming. It would link with that range of recreation, leisure and educational purposes that have been central to the expansion of tourism, and with the survival of local communities. Unfortunately for consumers their interests hardly rate with the juggernaut of Directorate General VI (Agriculture) and the compulsory expenditures to which it has title.

The CAP remains, embedded like some Jurassic fossil in Articles 38–45 of the Rome Treaty, untouched by the Single Act and Maastricht. Reform has been slow, grudging. Consumers cannot realize their economic power until they can penetrate the diaphanous unrealities of CAP policy. Simply to follow the complexities of the Irish beef scandal of the Haughey/Reynolds era in Ireland is to see how the intervention process damages consumer interests, distorts markets, and unsettles agricultural producers outside the Community.[8] The day has not yet come when consumer interests gain co-equality with those of this most powerful producer lobby.

The Utilities

In theory, the process of market liberalization now being applied with vigour to Europe's major utilities of energy and communications should be reducing oligopolistic producer power and widening the choice and relative strength of the citizen/consumer. But that is not how things have turned out. Consumer empowerment will only come from improved access, better quality standards, effective regulation, transparency of pricing and prompt redress. In Britain this has led to the development, within the framework of market mechanisms, of new patterns of independent regulation in the public interest – Office of Telecommunications (OFTEL), Office of Gas Supply (OFGAS) and the rest – where competition does not naturally exist.

The new quasi-monopolies are concerned with eliminating their competitors and enriching their corporate élites – neither likely to increase or enhance consumer power. It is the regulators who have come to the fore in the argument about how prices should be fixed and particular services licensed. The bizarre example of a privatized local monopoly, Yorkshire Water, using the courts to limit its customers' access to the service for which it charges them, despite the fact that it wastes more water through unrepaired leaks than do they, indicates the strength of the case for vigorous regulation.

Within the Community, there is no rational and efficient energy market in gas and electricity, nor is there proper co-operation between member states to ensure universal

---

[8] See 'Green Hearts', Anne Enright's review of *Meanwhile Back at the Ranch: The Politics of Irish Beef* by Fintan O'Toole, *London Review of Books*, 3 August 1995

service and security of supply. Member states have adopted different tax and subsidy schemes, and different approaches to the question of energy efficiency in the environmental context.

In the liberalization of telecommunications, moreover, the dominant players in the Council and the Commission have argued for self-regulation and a light touch, so that the chances of European investment in this vast new global market are not imperilled. What has not been addressed is the relative strength of the consumer/viewer if 'internal plurality' in the various states is ignored. If major suppliers are allowed to become dominant in their own national markets, viewers may find themselves locked into systems which they would prefer to abandon. The continual debate about conditional access systems for digital broadcasting clearly illustrates the way in which, as the old telecommunications monopolies are broken up, consumer choice needs to be protected in the agglomeration of powerful new media players, who have scant interest in the provision of universal services. And the Commission has shied away from any intervention to protect plural choice in Italy, where the dominant media player has also been the dominant player in government.

Summary

How can greater economic justice for the consumer be achieved? The key priorities are to seek the high ground of best practice, minimizing the exclusions which proliferate in the directives, properly monitoring their enforcement, and integrating consumer interest into all the relevant European legislation, including agriculture. It means extending the principle of appropriate and independent regulation by mandatory provision and establishing the principles of universal service and transparent pricing in public services.

Testing out every one of these cannot be done without the second of the 1975 principles: access to justice for those who seek redress.

Access to Redress

The Commission has acknowledged that without equal conditions of sale throughout the Community, and simple, inexpensive and effective forms of redress the single market will have no credibility.

In 1993 the Commission published two complementary discussion documents; a Green Paper on EU-wide Guarantees and After-Sales Service which explored the provision of equal conditions of sale in an integrated market, and a Green Paper on Access to Justice which tackles the specific question of redress. It has also promised, in 1995, a directive on the mutual recognition of collective action, and a communication on other measures concerning access to justice, including networks for the exchange of information. The Green Paper on Guarantees had set out alternative routes to establish guarantees that would be honoured in other member states, either through a more effective policing of the existing competition rules, or voluntary ground rules, or a European Guarantee Fund with opting-in for traders as a commercial guarantee. The Green Paper also looked at the possibility of a legal Guarantee, enforceable in statute if the conditions could be established by minimum harmonization.

The Green Paper on Access to Justice surveyed the problem of Europe's multifarious languages, legal systems and consumer information sources, identifying six areas for urgent action. They were:

Protecting the Citizen as Consumer

- The need to facilitate court actions from other states in the legal system of any member state
- The cost of funding such actions
- The exchange of information
- National Ombudsmen schemes all funded within their national industrial sectors, but conforming to minimum EU-wide criteria
- Co-operation between arbitration bodies
- Improved cross-border information on rights of access

None of the above can be brought to the point of resolution without the provision of judicial redress, for individual as well as collective interest disputes. Individual disputes are on the increase, as consumers find themselves in conflict with cross-border providers of property, tourism and transport, sale and repair of cars and domestic appliances, and banking and insurance operations. A Eurobarometer survey has shown a clear demand for action in this area: over 80% of consumers wanted identical protection throughout the member states.[9]

The European Consumers' Organization (commonly called BEUC after its French title[10]) has taken up this cause, proposing a network of specialized information centres able to provide advice on the vagaries of the different legal systems and the provision of legal aid, backed by a central co-ordinating agency.

As the Consumers in Europe Group, an umbrella body for UK professional, statutory and voluntary organizations interested in European consumer policy, has recently pointed out, it is quite wrong that the trader and producer, having taken advantage of the integrated market, should

[9] *Le Marché Unique des Consommateurs*, Eurobarometer Survey, November 1992.
[10] Bureau Européen des Unions de Consommateurs.

deny the same mobility of action to the consumer. The place of purchase should be irrelevant in the single market to the right to buy a product or service, with effective legal redress if it is defective. An EU-wide guarantee, with a baseline established by harmonization, would not achieve everything the best-protected member states already have in their own jurisdiction, but it would advance their citizens' cause in cross-border disputes, and provide a substantial advance for those whose national consumer rights are less protected.

Protection of Health and Safety

The third objective set out in 1975, protection of health and safety, has been a central priority throughout and as a result has achieved more. European legislation has concentrated on standardization, liability, certification, risk control and preventive action. Standardization, the butt of many Euro-tales, has led to a mass of directives on the preparation, labelling and contents of foodstuffs and manufactured products. The emphasis on product safety has widened out to current proposals for common safety and test procedures, especially of motor vehicles and coaches. A single registration system for medicinal products is also projected, with the European Agency for the Evaluation of Medicinal Products set up in London.

Liability
Product liability has been identified as a Community priority for two decades, unlike services, which came into the reckoning much later. The 1985 directive on Product Liability established a system which allows all victims (not only the contracting partners) to appeal against the producer for damages causing death, bodily injury or damage

to property. It excludes compensation for damage to the product itself and non-material consequences. Although admirable in theory, the directive has been dogged by failures to implement it and by the exclusion of cross-border disputes which remain the hole in the heart of liability law. There is no fully harmonized system, and the actual rights and obligations attached to product liability remain confused; producers are unsure of their obligations between one member state and another, consumers find their right of redress obscured. The position regarding liability for defective services is worse. Draft directives submitted in the 1990s have all been neutralized by heavy producer lobbying.

It will take strong pressure on the Commission to toughen the product liability regulations to provide the consumer with a protective package that would deliver what has been promised in the past. To achieve this, the existing directive would need to embrace products now excluded (notably agricultural), incorporate tough penalties and a response to the producers' 'state of the art' defence for defects, consider the effect of opt-outs within individual States where a producer has become insolvent or has vanished, and examine the impact of development hazards. It would also need to be linked to a comprehensive directive on liability for services.

Certification and Monitoring

Certification and monitoring have also promised more than they have delivered. The EC Certification mark was promoted by the Commission as a means of improving quality through universal conformity with technical standards. Those who take it as a mark of higher levels of safety and quality, however, are nonplussed to find that it is a measure of the minimum standards imposed by European legislation in, for example, energy efficiency, and in no sense a 'best buy'. The monitoring system intended to produce an early-warning system for dangerous products may in time become more effective, especially if it can cover products imported into the Community (Poland, an applicant state, is an example of a new trading partner which has no independent product liability law of its own). Also the monitoring needs to take into account those products deemed to be intrinsically dangerous by some member states, but regarded with tolerance elsewhere, such as flammable furniture.

Preventative action

The consumer stands to gain most, in the long run, from a comprehensive system of preventive action in the field of health and safety. An ambitious programme of Community action on health promotion, information, education and training is planned for 1996–2000. A wider understanding of nutritional principles, health and education has merit, although the Community would be taken more seriously if it were not simultaneously providing 1132 million ecu for tobacco-growers in Europe![11] The problem with much of this activity has been its inability to include consumer organizations, press and public in the rationale of the standardization process. As a result, labelling, for example, has often descended into a fiasco. There are 15,000 food items in a large supermarket. Few carry clear indications of content and attendant risk. The Nutrition Labelling Directive requires manufacturers to set out energy, protein, carbohydrate and fat contents, but not in an accessible, jargon-free form. Consumers receive muddled messages when clarity should prevail.

[11] Commission estimates of tobacco subsidy, Summer 1995.

Probably the most effective preventive health measures initiated by the Community have not been under the consumer rubric, but in the general field of environmental protection. The water we use has to conform to standards set by the Drinking Water and Bathing Water directives. The former protects all residents as customers of the British water authorities and provides standards for the new regulators, the National Rivers Authority, Office of Water Services (OFWAT) and the Drinking Water Inspectorate, although its impact has been, so to speak, watered down in transposition by the Department of the Environment. In the words of the environmental campaigner Nigel Haigh, 'The EC Legislation over the last twenty years has been the single biggest driving force for improving environmental standards in the UK. [It] sets numerical standards by deadlines in a way which you don't find in British legislation. Britain's self-image is that it only signs up to things which it obeys, and so it actually has to fulfil these obligations.'[12] However, there is still a long way to go in the face of growing pressure to dismantle environmental legislation in the name of simplicity.

Information and Education

The role of information provision – the fourth of the 1975 objectives – is especially crucial in Britain, where misinformation about the Community abounds. Citizens need to know when and how their consumer rights are being entrenched and extended, and equally when they are being

---

[12] N. Haigh, quoted in Ward, Buller and Lowe, 'Implementing European Environmental Policy at the Local Level: The British Experience with Water Quality Directives', Newcastle University, 1995.

lost in an excess of bureaucratic zeal.

The record since Maastricht has been patchy. The budget for consumer education has not been generous. A formal commitment to the introduction of consumer information centres has thus far only brought ten into operation. Consumer education in schools and further education has remained a matter of pilot schemes for the few and pious exhortation for the many. The budget has been used for radio and general advertising in the member states, when it could be more specifically linked to the existing resources and expertise of consumer organizations. The training of schoolteachers and the provision of appropriate classroom aids would bring home to the next generations the reasons for the Community's emphasis on consumer protection.

Young people need to know how protective legislation is drawn up, and be aware of the wider consequences of western purchasing power. Consumers ought to know who gains and who loses under the CAP and the sugar agreements, just as they ought to know the conditions which delivered the goods and services they subsequently enjoy.

If, as is alleged, a footwear manufacturer sub-contracts its work to say, Indonesia, where workers may earn only 10% of the retail value of the product they make, or if European airlines operate their computer reservation services through high-skill, low-wage staff in India, then this too will form part of the calculations of consumer choice which the citizen will want to consider.

Representation and Participation

The possibility of asserting the true voice of the consumer is also central to the fifth and final 1975 objective – consultation. The current consultation procedures give poor assessments of costs and benefits of particular sets of regulations and include producer representatives with much better rights of access in the network of consultative and advisory committees than consumers have. Consumers need to know the basis, rationale, implementation and methods of risk assessment used to draw up the measures intended for their protection.

It is commonplace for European parliamentarians waiting for a sight of a draft directive in the consumer field to discover that the producer lobbies concerned have known its every detail for months. MEPs soon learn that there is no safe haven from lobbyists in the European Parliament. They are everywhere. They are insistent. Too many parliamentarians can speak five languages, but are unable to say 'no' in any of them. A register of lobbying activities as well as MEPs' consultancies is long overdue. The problem is made worse by the fact that the consumer interest as such is not part of the initial trawl of opinions when the policy of other directorates is being formed, neither in trade, competition, transport, agriculture nor environment. Yet the consumer has a legitimate interest in all of these.

The Case for a Pro-Active Consumer Policy

Labour's domestic agenda has given the representation and protection of consumers its proper place, with a call for a Consumers' Charter to establish a common framework of rights for consumers across Europe. The Party of European Socialists (PES) is in the forefront of the campaign for treaty amendments that will help make this a reality. It will require persistence and dedication of a kind entirely lacking in a xenophobic Tory Government which has taken a *de minimis* approach to European initiatives. That includes the commitment to build on Article 129a of the Treaty, and to think hard about the way in which it has been frustrated by a clamour about subsidiarity. And above all the PES and Labour should break the linkage which left consumer protection measures legitimate only if they contributed to internal market policy. Information about products was prioritized over establishing the liability of producers and suppliers, together with access to justice for the plaintiffs in such cases.

Until recently there was a lack of political will in the Commission. The old Consumer Policy Service did not have the weight to confront the powerful directorates. The new DG XXIV can be a force for changing the balance. The fate of the draft directive on Distance Selling – butchered by the British in the Council – will be an early indication of the new approach. It will include the involvement of the European Parliament at every stage where the Commission's attempt to assert consumer protection is put in an armlock by an aggressive minority in the Council.

One of the happy consequences of the recent enlargement was that the Swedes in particular have begun to make official papers available to the public. The Council of Ministers gives no sign that it has even heard of the principles of open government – that 'transparency' which its own opaque practices so mock. The deliberations and decisions of the Council remain shrouded in secrecy. The member states must themselves do better. It will be an early test of the new European Parliamentary Ombudsman, the Finnish Socialist Jacob Soderman, to establish a right of access to all documents held by the European institutions.

The same applies to the abuse of the principle of subsidiarity, in a field where international action to make consumer protection effective is critical. The general premise of Maastricht, that matters will only be pursued at EU level if they cannot be effectively carried through at national, regional or local level, is unexceptional in itself, but needs to be dynamically and not negatively interpreted. Decision-making should always be at the optimum level. Distortions of competition rooted in differences of laws and regulations, failures of implementation in cross-border contracts and transactions, lack of consultation with consumers: all can be covered up by the excuse of subsidiarity. The CEG have called for a fair and transparent test of the criteria to be set for the application of subsidiarity, on a case by case basis, open to review by the European Parliament and the Court of Justice. This should be supported. The European Parliament has its own role to play, with enlarged co-decision powers and the power to set an example by the openness of its own proceedings.

During future revisions, the interests of the consumer will need to be carried forcefully into the deliberations. To ensure the promotion of balanced and sustainable economic and social progress, the treaty should be amended to include the promotion of consumer interests, fully integrated with all other Community policies.

The abolition of restraints on trade and competition should be linked with the caveat that such measures must not result in a net reduction in consumer benefit. Article 129a should be substantially amended to assert the centrality of consumer concerns to all the Community's policies, the guaranteeing of consumer rights in:

- Economic Justice
- Access to Redress
- Protection of Health and Safety
- Information and Education
- Representation and Participation

Had Article 129a been vigourously interpreted in the first place, there would be no need for a comprehensive revision.

These are the principles of 1975, enshrined in the treaty, together with a commitment to enforce directives pursuant to these rights equally throughout the member states. Such a commitment would fit well with Labour's national aims of consumer protection. The Party wants the rebuilding of a proper consumer advice system, vigorous support for a revitalized consumer and trading standards service, locally and nationally, simplified standards of customer contracts, performance standards, labelling, and product liability. It wants to remove the flaccid fumbling of the OFT and the Monopolies and Mergers Commission (MMC), and replace them with an effective body to guard the public interest.

There is a genuine consumer interest to be sustained across the Community, upheld and enforced by member states committed, as a Labour Britain would be, to fair competition consistent with consumer rights and not superimposed upon them. The Europe of legend, lurking over our crisps, ginger beer and mushy peas, has too often given Brussels a bad name for misplaced standardization. It needs to realize that harmonization will only produce harmony if each stage is carried through in an appropriate manner; otherwise overzealous metricators and fanatical labellers will do more harm than good. The Europe of reality has to be a people's Europe, giving its citizens what they want and need only after hearing what they have to say, but then able to use national bodies to implement agreed measures of protection firmly and rigorously. Like the Fabian tortoise, consumer law needs to have the reputation that when it strikes, it strikes hard. Labour has the potential to offer, and Europe is the context in which it can be carried through.

DAVID MARTIN
Power to the People

As a democratic socialist party, Labour has always acted by arguing for its policies, putting its programme to the people and then campaigning for power through democratic elections. This is the way Labour operates at local and national level. However, Europe is different. Although people are increasingly governed by and from Europe, there is no European government as such.

Transnational problems need supranational solutions. One of the key differences between the nationalist right and the internationalist left on European policy is that the right, whilst professing to protect the sovereignty of member states, does not want to place any curbs on international capitalism. At a European level, the right do not want any democratic power that could challenge multinational capital or redistribute the wealth created by the people of Europe.

The challenge facing Labour is how to engage constructively in Europe and deal with problems which require a European solution without relinquishing the power to act at home.

The Democratic Deficit

The puzzle at the heart of the European question is how to decrease the 'democratic deficit'; the fact that power has passed from member state parliaments to Europe but is not being controlled there by the democratically elected representatives of the people. The way to answer the conundrum of the 'democratic deficit' in Europe is by giving 'power to the people'. This is the only solution for democratic socialists.

It should not be Labour's programme to set up a European government, but Labour should certainly aim to make the decisions which are taken at the European level more democratic and open. People need to know how decisions are being made in Europe, by whom and how these representatives can be replaced if they are not fulfilling the wishes of the people.

The 'democratic deficit' cannot be solved by repatriating power back to the member states. In many cases, member states are no longer equipped to deal with challenges such as those which have emerged following the end of the Cold War. Equally, member states acting alone cannot cope with damage to the environment, or the impact of the information technology revolution and its repercussions for employment.

Three Challenges – Policy, Credibility, Enlargement

At the European level, an incoming Labour government will have to deal with three crucial problems.

Firstly, we need to improve the EU's ability to deliver on key policy objectives, both within the Union and internationally. At the moment, the three-pillar structure means that foreign policy and justice and home affairs are outside the European Community's influence. In addition to this, the existence of unanimity has been seen to restrict action – for example, in the areas of unemployment and social policy. These are Labour's issues. If the Union cannot deliver on them, what is Europe for? Labour should boldly campaign for an end to the three-pillar structure and an increase in qualified majority voting. I believe these changes would be right for the British people, for Europe and for the wider world. Labour has the enthusiasm and determination to deal with unemployment and social policy, but will need institutional means at the European level. Internationally, Europe has not been punching its weight: the three-pillar structure has restricted our ability to take effective action in the former Yugoslavia, or measures to tackle drugs-smuggling and international crime. Labour's traditional internationalism must reassert itself through the European Union. We must give a lead in the area of common foreign and security policy.

Secondly, Labour will have to regain the support of citizens for European co-operation and integration. There is presently a legitimacy gap between the institutions of the European Union and the people. I believe this can be attributed to the complexity of the structures and the intricacy of the decision-making processes. People will not give their loyalty to what they do not understand.

Thirdly, Labour will be faced with the imminent enlargement of the Union; an institutional structure designed for six but already struggling to cope with fifteen members. Europe simply cannot accommodate twenty-seven or more members without a radical overhaul of its existing structures. But rather than seeing this as a threat, a Labour government should see enlargement as an opportunity to deepen the structures of the Union in a way that will allow it to deal with the core issues of peace and prosperity. Widening and deepening are part of the same process; they are not mutually exclusive.

Merging the Pillars

The 'pillar structure' set up by the Maastricht Treaty on European Union has been a failure. Since foreign and security policy and justice and home affairs (the second and third pillars) are outside the legal framework of the European Communities, they have not been subject to either the stimulation or the checks and balances guaranteed by the involvement of the European Commission, Parliament and Court of Justice. I believe that all three pillars should be merged and replaced with a single Community structure. This would bring more coherence to the decision-making process by ending the artificial division between trade and development on the one hand, and foreign and security policy on the other. It would place justice and home affairs back where they belong among the other aspects of free movement, and it would give the Court of Justice a true role.

The merging of the pillar structure would enhance the roles of the Commission, Parliament and the Court of Justice in matters of vital importance to the citizen. It would also make the Community more coherent to the outside world. At present, the Union is sometimes represented by the Commission and sometimes by the Council in international affairs.

A Citizens' Europe

Problems over the ratification of the Maastricht Treaty made it clear that the process of European integration is at risk if it is seen to be too remote from everyday needs. Concerns about Europe being centralized and technocratic abound. It is essential that practical steps be taken by Labour to bring the European Union closer to the citizen and vice versa. A first step could be to ensure that the concept of European citizenship be given greater meaning. This would tie-in with Labour's programme of democratic renewal at home. The concept of European Union citizenship introduced by the Maastricht Treaty was a significant but limited development. In concrete terms, it provided for citizens to be represented by any European Union embassy abroad and for electors to vote in their member state of residence in local and European elections. The possibility exists of extending this provision to member state general/parliamentary elections.

The European Parliament has for many years supported the principle of accession by the European Community to the Council of Europe's Convention on Human Rights and Fundamental Freedoms. Such a move would ensure that the Community was subject to the same human-rights monitoring procedures under the European Convention on Human Rights as member states. This is a cause which could be championed by Labour at the European level and would mirror Labour's commitments at UK level. If Labour were also to advocate that the European Union should add the rights contained in the Social Chapter and the Joint Declaration Against Racism and Xenophobia to any new treaty, as well as a citizen's rights to information on European Union matters, we would in effect be arguing for the most progressive constitution in the world. With the promise of such guaranteed rights, the people of Europe would have the most positive reasons for wanting the integration of the European Union to progress.

Open decision-making procedures are essential in any democratic society. Labour is committed to a Freedom of Information Act at home. One of the most important ways in which European Union decision-making could be made more accessible to its citizens would be to make the whole process of government much more open. The European Council of Ministers should cease to make laws behind closed doors and should meet in public when acting in its legislative capacity. The public must be given greater access to European Union documents. If we are to give power to the people at the European level, we must maintain the potential for all European Union citizens to be elected to the European Parliament and to take part in its debates. There should be no reduction in the number of official European Union languages.

Another strategy for bringing the European Union closer to the citizen is the introduction of the concept of 'subsidiarity'. The principle of 'subsidiarity' was introduced to ensure that political decisions within the European Union were exercised as closely as possible to its citizens and to ensure that decisions which are best taken at European Union level do not go further than necessary. Institutional reforms are not needed in this area.

The Maastricht Treaty also attempted to make the working of the European Union more relevant and explicable to its citizens by creating the Committee of the Regions, which allows local and regional government to feed their expertise into the process of European integration. With the creation of a Scottish Parliament, a Welsh Assembly and different bodies to represent the regions of England, a Labour government could make an important contribution to this.

Enlargement

As we move from a possible Labour strategy for bringing the European Union even closer to its citizens to the third challenge which will face a Labour government – that of enlargement – we must confront the issue which will necessitate the most profound changes. It has become increasingly difficult for fifteen member states to pass legislation when a national veto is in operation. It will be almost impossible with the twenty-seven-plus members we expect to have by early next century. Radical solutions will be necessary if the European Union is to satisfy the aspirations of its people. Without major institutional changes, the European Union will degenerate into a big club for big business; which is exactly the position that the Eurosceptics of the right are working towards.

Applications for membership of the European Union from Malta and Cyprus are currently on the table. Poland, Hungary, the Czech Republic, Slovakia, Bulgaria and Romania have associate agreements. The three Baltic states – Latvia, Lithuania and Estonia – and Slovenia are waiting in the wings. Nobody is arguing that these countries should not be allowed into the European Union. Membership is important for the former Eastern European communist states as is would confirm their hard-won democratic status, just as it did for Greece, Spain and Portugal. One of the arguments against the old European Economic Community used to be that it represented only part of Europe. We now have a chance to remedy that objection but we will need new institutional means in order to do so.

One result of enlargement will be the numbers game. If we are to be pragmatic, we shall have to find a way to accommodate the interests of both large and small member states efficiently. The principle of equality of treatment among member states is of particular importance in the collegiate Commission, where Union rather than member state interests must be defended, and we should continue to have at least one Commissioner per member state. As far as representation in the European Parliament is concerned, a review of the number of MEPs per member state is required. The European Parliament has already stated that there should be an upper limit of 700 members and that the number should be revised every ten years on the basis of the latest population census. There should also be a review of numbers at the European Court of Justice and the European Court of Auditors.

Qualified Majority Voting

To invite these countries in and then allow everyone to sit around the table clutching a veto would lead to the tyranny of the minority. We would only be able to move as fast as the slowest, and consequently would see no more social or environmental improvements. We would be reduced to the lowest common denominator. That is not what the people of Europe want. On as many issues as is reasonable, we must move to majority voting. That is, after all, the way democracy works. A special system of qualified majority voting has already evolved within the Council of Ministers to enhance democracy. [1]

[1] Qualified majority voting is a weighted system of voting introduced into the procedures of the Council of Ministers to produce more efficient decision-taking. The present line-up of voting strengths is: Austria 4, Belgium 5, Denmark 3, Finland 3, France 10, Germany 10, Greece 5, Ireland 3, Italy 10, Luxembourg 2, Netherlands 5, Portugal 5, Spain 8, Sweden 4, UK 10. The qualified majority required to adopt legislation in a Union of 15 member states is 62 out of 87. The blocking minority is 26 votes. It sometimes takes at least 10 states to pass the qualified majority.

With the proposed enlargement, if weighted voting is retained at the present level, there could be a situation where 47% of the population of the European Union is represented by 71% of the vote. There must be a reform of the present system in favour of countries with larger populations, or the introduction of 'reinforced' or 'double' majorities which would mean that legislation would require majorities of member states to be backed up by majorities of the total European Union population.

The present Conservative government's opposition to an increase in qualified majority voting is hypocritical. Mrs Thatcher's government voted in favour of abandoning the national veto and accepting more majority voting when she signed the Single European Act. John Major's government voted for an increase in qualified majority voting when he signed the Maastricht Treaty. They did so because they wanted more efficient decision-making. The same argument applies to the decisions to be made concerning enlargement.

Reforming the Institutions

At the institutional level, Labour could become the champion of a more efficient, open and accountable European Union. Labour should make it clear that we do not want to transfer any new powers to Europe. Our aim will be to bring those powers which are exercised at the European level under democratic control. With regard to the existing institutions, it is important that a Labour government argues for:

- the European Commission's current role and independence to be reasserted
- independent agencies to be be better co-ordinated and

controlled at European Union level
- the Council and Parliament to be established as equals in all fields of European Union legislative and budgetary competence
- the Commission, Parliament, Court of Justice and Court of Auditors to play their proper role in all areas which are primarily subject to intergovernmental decision-making
- the European Court of Justice to have the full means to ensure the respect for European Union laws
- the European Investment Bank to be made more accountable to European Union institutions.

Nothing turns voters off so much as seeing their own actions downgraded and top posts carved up in horse-trading behind closed doors. These are the practices new Labour is determined to root out at home, and the same rigorous principles should be applied in Europe. The débâcle over the election of Jacques Delors' successor as President of the European Commission brought the whole European Union into disrepute. This must never be repeated. In future, the President of the Commission should be elected by the European Parliament – the directly elected representatives of the people at European level – from a list of names put forward by the European Council. The rest of the Commission should then be put together by agreement between the President and the member state governments before coming to the Parliament for final investiture as a college.

Parliaments Working Together

Democratic scrutiny of European legislation could be greatly enhanced by more co-operation between European and member state parliaments. The member state parliaments and the European Parliament should act in a complementary fashion.

Direct democratic scrutiny, at the appropriate level and in an appropriate form, must be allowed for all significant European Union decisions. All treaty articles, including those in the second and third pillars, should be reviewed with this standard in mind. Democratic control will be best achieved by partnership between the European Parliament and member state parliaments, and not through conflict between them as to who is responsible for what. We have a common interest in the furtherance of democracy.

Rationalizing Procedures

For the European Parliament to play its full role, in a way that the public can understand, the present procedures must be rationalized and simplified. A major step in improving ordinary citizens' understanding of the workings of the European Union would be to simplify and reduce the number of decision-making procedures from an astonishing twenty-seven to only three: co-decision, assent and consultation. The co-decision procedure (whereby the Commission and the Parliament must be in agreement) should apply to all areas in which legislation is adopted by the Council – at the very least, in all cases where majority voting applies. The Council is there to represent the interests of member states; the European Parliament should represent the democratic rights of the European electorate as a whole. No European law should be passed without the joint consent of Council and Parliament. The assent procedure should be restricted to treaty revisions, international agreements, enlargements and adjustments to EU resources.

The consultation procedure should be restricted to decisions concerning common foreign policy and security. The European Parliament should also be given an enhanced right of initiative. It is important that MEPs have procedures that allow them to take action on behalf of their constituents. Such reforms would make the whole decision-making system seem less esoteric and give genuine power to the people.

If the European Union is to function efficiently with an increased membership, Labour must champion a further extension of majority voting in the Council. For certain restricted areas, such as constitutional issues, treaty amendments, own resources, enlargement, a common electoral system, and decisions taken outside the Union's formal area of competence, we should continue to advocate retention of the veto. On the other hand, in the area of foreign policy and security, it is important that the Union should take decisions by majority vote, with the safeguard that no member state should be forced to take part in action it does not want to be involved in. (At the same time, the understanding would be that it would not prevent others from acting together.) Common foreign policy and the future security and defence arrangements of the Union are likely to become increasingly central issues. Labour should not shy away from this issue. We should play to our strengths. The UK has one of the most talented Foreign Offices in the world and a professional army, navy and air force second to none. A British Labour government should play a central role in the formation of this area of policy. We must not allow ourselves to be absent when important decisions are being taken, as we were with the Common Agricultural Policy: or standing on the sidelines, as the Tories were, over the future of the European Central Bank. Labour should be at the heart of Europe, influencing the collective decisions in the interests of the people.

Taking the Left Turn

This last proposal brings us to the core of the argument between left and right over Europe: should we have a more integrated European Union which would allow for the socialist principle of redistribution; or a more intergovernmental European Union which would make such a move more difficult, if not impossible? Intergovernmentalism would not allow the redistribution of wealth created by the Single European Market, nor would it enable the creation of European Union-wide social welfare, or any of the other benefits socialists would like to achieve for the people of Europe. Nor would intergovernmentalism allow for the control of capital flows or the regulation of multinational companies. Individual member states are no longer strong enough to control capital speculators or to curb the activities of multinational companies.

This can only be achieved by co-ordinated effort at European and global level. One of the prime reasons that right-wing thinkers oppose a more integrated Europe is that it would have the power to control companies and individuals and stop them playing one country off against another.

We are approaching a crossroads of enormous significance in the history of the European Union. One route could lead us towards unfettered consumer capitalism, creating a society of alienated, disenfranchised individuals. The other road leads to a society where individual freedom and prosperity are combined with collective activity to create community and social welfare for all.

In a continent of great diversity which has seen two world wars this century, Labour can contribute towards an ideal of peace and prosperity which could provide a model for the rest of the world. It is time for the left in Britain to argue for the positive integration of Britain into the heart of a democratic European Union. Then, and only then, can we play our full part in that great venture that will steer the European Union on a middle course: a third way between the discredited economic determinism and command economies of the former Soviet Union on the one hand, and the competitive capitalism of the USA and Japan on the other. This is the route Labour should be taking in Europe.

GARY TITLEY
Developing the Brussels–Westminster Axis

The theme of David Martin's chapter is 'power to the people'. That empowerment is Labour's overriding priority in the European debate. The changes in the way the European Union makes its decisions should be aimed at making the EU more accessible and more easily understood by its citizens and so enhance its democratic legitimacy.

There is one aspect which stands out as an essential prerequisite if we are really to give power to the people. We need to review the way we think about European affairs and in particular the relationship between Westminster and the European Parliament.

We have to stop thinking that the Westminster parliament and the European Parliament are in competition. They are in fact two sides of the same coin – the democratic accountability of the forces which govern our lives. They should be working together in pursuit of that common end. Giving more power to the European Parliament enhances proper democratic scrutiny of the exercise of sovereignty already ceded to Brussels, rather than taking power away from Westminster.

The EU now has more competencies than it had under the original Treaty of Rome. The Council of Ministers can make some decisions by majority voting. These extra powers have to be monitored. Yet national parliaments find their ministers hide behind the anonymity of the Council of Ministers when called to account for their actions. Meanwhile, the European Parliament is often frustrated in its quest for accountability by the limitation of its powers. There is a democratic black hole.

Effective interparliamentary co-operation has to be a Labour priority. It will involve strengthening our own structures, but mainly look at how Westminster scrutinizes European legislation and how that process can be strengthened through close links with MEPs.

In terms of reviewing its own structures, the party has already strengthened its policy co-ordination. The Deputy Leader now liaises between the NEC, Westminster, and the European Parliamentary Labour Party and the Party of European Socialists. Each front-bench team has designated a member responsible for European aspects of the portfolio. That person is also a member of the front-bench European Co-ordinating Committee. The EPLP has liaison people appointed for each of the European Parliament's committees. They are also members of the appropriate Westminster front-bench team. The leader of the EPLP is also a member of the NEC and is invited from time to time to attend shadow cabinet meetings. Shadow cabinet members also attend EPLP meetings.

This structure is in marked contrast to the totally divided nature of the Tory approach to European policy-making. It is important that the party works now on developing and strengthening these relationships so that they can be carried forward into government. In government, co-operation will be essential. The problem is that even the most perfect working relationships are likely to be pulled apart by the institutional divide that separates MPs from MEPs. That divide is symbolized by the fact that Westminster allows

MEPs into the Central Lobby and the Committee Corridor but no further. MEPs might be seen but are certainly not heard. In such circumstances, how can we work together to ensure that we get the best deal for ordinary people in Britain?

We cannot continue like this. The European debate is dominated by misconceptions, ignorance and downright mischief – so much so that a coherent discussion about the future of Europe becomes impossible. Yet arcane rules undermine our ability to co-operate in doing something about it. No wonder our citizens are confused, suspicious and increasingly hostile towards the EU. This must change. The two Parliaments must work together.

The Maastricht Treaty brought the issue of interparliamentary co-operation into sharp focus. Firstly, the treaty created two pillars of intergovernmental co-operation – foreign and security policy and justice and home affairs. These are a grey area when it comes to parliamentary scrutiny, as with all areas of intergovernmental co-operation. It is vital that both national parliaments and the European Parliament co-operate in calling ministers to account, regardless of the outcome of the IGC. Secondly, a declaration annexed to the treaty called for:

- The exchange of information between national parliaments and the European Parliament to be stepped up
- Governments to ensure that national parliaments receive Commission proposals for legislation in good time for information or possible examination
- The stepping up of contacts between national parliaments and the European Parliament through regular meetings and reciprocal facilities

In a separate declaration, the treaty also invited the

European and national parliaments to meet as necessary as a Conference of the Parliaments (or 'assizes').

In fact, in 1991 the European Parliament had already launched a programme of initiatives under five headings:

- Invitations to the European Affairs Committee of each national parliament to meet the European Parliament
- Participation by members of the national parliaments in meetings of the counterpart Committees of the European Parliament
- Meetings between European Parliament and national parliament rapporteurs dealing with the same issues
- Round tables with all counterpart Committees of the national parliaments
- Opportunities for MEPs to give evidence to national parliaments

As a result, there has been a marked change in the volume and character of interparliamentary meetings. These meetings have ensured growing awareness of common interests across the parliaments of the EU. For example, it was the joint discussion at the Civil Liberties Committee in 1993 on the home and judicial affairs pillar of the Maastricht Treaty that made all parliaments aware of the lack of democratic control in this area, and prompted a debate on how to deal with this problem.

On top of these contacts, more formal parliamentary liaison bodies have been formed. The Conference of Presidents of the European Parliament and of the national parliaments meets once every six months, while the Conference of European Affairs Committees of the national parliaments and the European Parliament (COSAC) meets every six months and discusses two or three specified issues.

Significantly, the one liaison body which has not worked has been the Conference of Parliaments foreseen in the

Maastricht Treaty. One suspects that this is because its very nature is so insubstantial. Liaison appears to work best where both sides have a specific agenda to work to on matters of mutual interest, rather than participating in a grand 'talking shop'. Labour should not advocate or support structures for their own sake. Legislators face enormous pressure and liaison work will only be successful and meaningful where concrete results can be achieved.

That liaison will have as its main reference point the way Westminster deals with EU matters and how this can be improved. It is all too easy for ministers to pass the buck, declining to give a full answer on the grounds that the matter is currently under discussion in the Council of Ministers. Yet when MEPs ask the same question of the Council, they may be told this is a matter for member governments and the Council cannot comment further. Thus information appears to have disappeared down a black hole. It is vital for MEPs and back-bench MPs to co-operate and shore up these gaps in the democratic process.

More specific scrutiny of EU legislation takes place in the Select Committee on European Legislation. It receives copies of Commission proposals, together with an Explanatory Memorandum prepared by the relevant government department, which provides information about the general effect of the document, its legal and policy implications, and any further relevant information. The Committee publishes a report on the documents considered, highlighting important issues and making any recommendations for further consideration by the House. Such further consideration is normally carried out by one of two European Standing Committees, which debates the matter and then draws up a resolution for the House. The government undertakes not to agree to Community legislative proposals ahead of parliamentary scrutiny.

This sounds a tight enough system, but how does it work in practice? In July 1993 an Efficiency Scrutiny Report, commissioned by Michael Heseltine, was published under the title 'Review of the Implementation and Enforcement of EC Law in the UK'. It was very critical:

> Many businesses complained that MPs show little interest in EC legislation until it is too late. We think this is mainly due to lack of awareness rather than lack of interest. We were told that as soon as an EC Commission proposal is tabled, the Netherlands parliament receives a brief which sets out the purpose of the directive, the type of legislative changes and problems which might be expected. The whole parliament has the opportunity to comment and thereby influence negotiating strategies. By contrast, in the UK, Explanatory Memoranda (EMs) are placed in the library of both houses and scrutiny is delegated to committees. Only a minority of proposals are recommended for debate in either House and only in exceptional circumstances do the committees call ministers for examination.

Furthermore, the report was critical of the government's Explanatory Memoranda, which it described as 'bland and drafted deliberately to obscure problems which might present difficulties for ministers'.

Clearly, whatever the theory, the practice of parliamentary scrutiny leaves a lot to be desired. Improving it has to be a priority for Labour and in doing this we can learn from other countries.

Another good example is Denmark. There, prime responsibility for European matters lies with the European Affairs Committee. The government forwards to the committee copies of all Commission proposals which are then registered and filed in the EU information centre in the

Folketing *and so are accessible to the general public*. The committee, however, mainly works from notes produced by the relevant Ministry concerning the Commission proposals. Ninety-five per cent of these notes are available to the public. The main items on the agenda of the committee are the Council meetings. The relevant minister outlines both the issues to be discussed and the government's position. A debate then takes place, after which the committee decides whether to endorse the government's approach or not. After the Council meeting, the minister responsible forwards to the committee the minutes of the meeting so that it can check the minister has followed the agreed line. On important matters of principle, a debate in the full Parliament may follow. The European Affairs Committee also liaises with the other committees of the Danish parliament. All papers are sent to the specialist committees and there is a regular exchange of information. A minister may appear before a specialist committee to discuss a European matter and then the committee may send a recommendation to the European Affairs Committee. The committees can hold hearings with MEPs, including joint hearings with the European Affairs Committee.

Some members of the European Affairs Committee are also members of the European Parliament. However, most parties do not allow this double membership. Co-operation with MEPs therefore takes place within the party structures. To assist this, all documents of the European Affairs Committee are forwarded to Danish MEPs. MEPs also sit on a European Council which has been set up to advise the European Affairs Committee along with representatives of groups with an interest in EU affairs, such as the Social Partners. The committee also follows the course of legislation through the European Parliament.

There are two other highly practical aspects worth noting. Firstly, the European Affairs Committee *meets on a Friday afternoon all year around* (except August), *even when the Folketing is not in session.* This enables it to follow the pace of Brussels and the legislative timetable of the European Parliament. One of the major problems with Westminster's scrutiny of EU legislation is that its timetable is so different from Brussels. Secondly, the Folketing has a representative in Brussels. He reports on the work of the European institutions.

It is clearly impossible to transplant one parliament's procedures into another. Labour must commit itself to a thorough review of Westminster's procedures based on best practice elsewhere. In particular, it should have the following objectives:

- the provision of more thorough information to MPs
- greater powers to the Select Committee on European Legislation
- ensuring that agendas of Council meetings can be discussed by the Select Committee before and after such meetings take place
- making greater parliamentary control over the operation of the second and third pillars a priority
- reviewing the timetable for parliamentary procedure so that it can keep better track of the Brussels timetable
- appointing a House of Commons official, to be based in Brussels, fulfilling the same function as the representative of the Folketing
- establishing a formal role for MEPs, possibly through the creation of an advisory subcommittee, as well as giving them greater access to Commons documentation.
- granting MEPs greater access to the facilities at Westminster
- facilitating greater access for the Select Committee to the European Parliament's places of work

- guaranteeing greater public access to EU documents
- committing itself to opposing secrecy when the Council is acting as a legislative body

By combining the framework for co-operation between Labour MEPs and MPs already in place with reform of European scrutiny procedures in Westminster and a more formal institutional link between the two sorts of MPs, the next Labour Government would be striking a practical blow for democratic accountability. That, as David Martin has set out, needs to be accompanied by measures to open up the Council of Ministers to greater democratic scrutiny, and to increase the European Parliament's powers over EU legislation and over the European Commission.

Together, these measures would create more openness and transparency. They would ensure the maximum input by Britain into EU policy and maximize the ability of a Labour Government to pursue policies for the benefit of ordinary citizens. Empowerment of the people would then be a reality.

Further reading

Adams, John, *Transport Planning*, RKP 1981
Bainbridge, Timothy and Teasdale, Anthony, *The Penguin Companion to the European Union*, Penguin 1995
Ball, R.M., *Local Authorities and Regional Policy: Attitudes, Representations and the Local Economy*, Paul Chapman 1995
Brown, Lester, *State of the World 1996*, W.W. Norton 1996
Collins, Richard, *Broadcasting and Audiovisual Policy in the European Single Market*, John Libby 1994
Collins, Richard, *Satellite Television in Western Europe*, John Libby 1994
Duff, Andrew, Pinder, John and Price, Roy (eds): *Maastricht and Beyond*, Routledge 1994
Ford, Glyn, *Evolution of a European*, Spokesman 1993
Ford, Glyn, *Fascist Europe*, Pluto 1992
Friends of the Earth, *Less Traffic, Better Towns* 1992
Gore, Al, *Earth in the Balance*, Earthscan 1992
Grant, Charles, *Delors: Inside the House that Jack Built*, Nicholas Brealey 1994
Hamer, Mick, *Wheels Within Wheels: A study of the road lobby*, RKP 1987
Harris, Geoff, *The Dark Side of Europe* (second edition), Edinburgh University Press 1994
Hilliard and Keith, *Global Broadcasting Systems*, Focal Press 1994
Holland, Stuart, *The European Imperative: Economic and*

Social Cohesion in the 1990s, Russell Press Ltd 1993

Hutton, Will, *The State We're In*, Vintage 1996

Jacobs, Francis, Corbett, Richard and Shackelton, Michael: *The European Parliament*, Longman 1994

Kapteyn, P.J.G. and Verloren van Themaat, P., *Introduction to the Law of the European Communities*, Kluwer 1990

Lodge, Juliet (ed), *The European Community and the Challenge of the Future*, Pinter 1989

MacDonald, Barrie, *Broadcasting in the UK*, Mansell 1993

Milliband, David (ed), *Reinventing the Left*, Polity Press 1994

Murphy, Phil and Caborn, Richard, *Regional Government in England – an economic imperative*, PAVIC Publications, Sheffield Hallam University 1995

Nugent, Neill, *The Government and Politics of the European Union*, Macmillan 1994

O'Keeffee, David and Twomey, Patrick M. (eds), *Legal Issues of the Maastricht Treaty*, Wiley Chancery 1994

O'Keohane, Robert and Hoffman, Stanley (eds), *The New European Community*, Westview 1991

Owen, Richard and Dynes, Michael: *The Times Guide to 1992*, Times 1990

Preston, Jill, *Regional Policy*, Spicers European Union Policy Briefings, Longman 1994

Royal Commission on Environmental Pollution, *Transport and the Environment*, HMSO 1994

Simpson, Anthony, *The Essential Anatomy of Britain: Democracy in Crisis*, Hodder & Stoughton 1992

Smith, Julie, *Voice of the People*, The Royal Institute of International Affairs 1995

Snyder, Francis, *Common Agricultural Policy of the European Communities*, Butterworth 1990

Sherlock, *Cities are Good for Us*, Paladin 1991

Swann, Dennis *The Economies of the Common Market: Integration in the European Union* (eighth edition), Penguin 1995

World Commission on Environment and Development, *Our Common Future*, OUP 1987